W9-API-056

EXPLORING

CELTIC

DRUIDISM

Ancient Magick and Rituals for Personal Empowerment

By

Sirona Knight

NEW PAGE BOOKS
A division of The Career Press, Inc.
Franklin Lakes, NJ

Copyright © 2001 by Sirona Knight

Exploring Celtic Druidism
Cover design by Diane Chin
Editing by Dianna Walsh
Typesetting by Eileen Munson
Illustrations by Colleen Koziara
Printed in the U.S.A. by Book-mart Press
To order this title, please call toll-free 1-800-CAREER-1 (NJ and Canada: 201-848-0310) to order using VISA or MasterCard, or for further information on books from Career Press.

The Career Press, Inc., 3 Tice Road, PO Box 687, Franklin Lakes, NJ 07417
www.careerpress.com
www.newpagebooks.com

Library of Congress Cataloging-in-Publication Data

Knight, Sirona, 1955-
    Exploring Celtic Druidism : ancient magick and rituals
for personal empowerment / by Sirona Knight.
        p. cm.
    Includes bibliographical references and index.
    ISBN 1-56414-489-5 (pbk.)
        1. Magic, Celtic. 2. Ritual. 3. Goddess religion. I. Title.

BF1622.C45 K65 2001
299'.16—dc21

                                        00-065375

For my Nana,

Jean "Gina" Berutti Avidano,

who was a Druid for 72 years.

And for my father,

Dr. John Morris Berutti,

who read me faery tales and

introduced me to the magic of myth

and folklore.

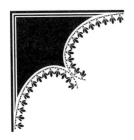

ACKNOWLEDGMENTS

I would especially like to thank and acknowledge Mike Lewis, my editor, for his friendship and continued faith in my writing. Brightest blessings and loving thanks to my agent, Lisa Hagan at Paraview, for her support, integrity, and friendship. I would also like to respectfully acknowledge and thank Ron Fry, my publisher at New Page Books, for having the insight and courage to print such an extraordinary new line of magical books. A special thank you to Stacey Farkas for doing such a great job with this book and for going beyond the call of duty.

Many thanks and heartfelt appreciation to my family and friends, especially Michael and Sky, for their eternal love, light, and laughter. You are the bright stars in my life! Respectful and loving thanks to the Celtic Goddesses and Gods, to my ancestors and descendants, and to the sacred land. I would also like to thank my teachers and the members of the College of the Sun in Chico, California, for sharing in the Great Adventure. And many blessings to John Nelson,

Melissa Dragich, and Heidi Ellen Robinson for their continued kindness and friendship. I would like to thank and acknowledge Donovan, R.J. Stewart, Josephine Stewart, Jean Markale, Loreena McKinnett, Maireid Sullivan, Alan Stivell, Aine Minogue, and Steve McDonald for talking with me and sharing their Celtic traditions. A special thank you to everyone at *Magical Blend* magazine, especially Michael Langevin, the editor and publisher, for his continued support and enthusiasm. I would also like to thank Dorothy Morrison, Patricia Telesco, A.J. Drew, Skye Alexander, Z. Budapest, Colleen Koziara, Raymond Buckland, Raven Grimassi, Phyllis Currot, Imajicka, and Boudica for their empowering friendship, and for helping the circle ever grow stronger. I would also like to acknowledge and thank all of you who are reading this book and are drawn to the Druid path. I wish each one of you perfect love and perfect peace. Blessed Be!

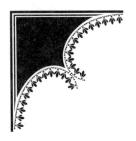

CONTENTS

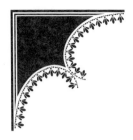

INTRODUCTION

The first time I came into contact with the teachings of Celtic Druidism at the age of 16, it felt like I'd come home. There was a familiarity to it that overwhelmed me and kindled my curiosity, and I set out on a quest to learn everything I could about the Celts and Druids.

On the night of my initiation into the Gwyddonic Druid tradition 15 years later, I had a profound spiritual experience that changed me. After the ritual, I felt like a new person, like someone who was suddenly whole again. Again, there was a haunting familiarity to it all.

I was raised Catholic, and I have vivid memories of astraling in church during Mass when the priests used to do the rituals in Latin. Not knowing what they were saying, I remember being transported to the ceiling and amongst the statuary by their intonation and cadence of their voices. Astraling was considerably better than just sitting there in the pews during services, trying to be quiet.

In many ways the gap between Catholicism and Celtic Druidism is not that wide. Each have priests who conduct rituals that bring in, and connect with, the Divine energy. Many of the Christian holidays were borrowed from the early Celtic Great Days, the two main ones being Yule, which became Christmas, and Hertha's Day or the Spring Equinox, which later became Easter. Because of this, the Celtic Druid rituals are akin to the Catholic rituals I experienced as a child.

One of the main differences between Celtic Druidism and Catholicism that really appeals to me is that there is a presiding High Priestess. Not only is there a High Priestess, but she is in the position of leadership and authority as the embodiment of the Goddess. This is why Celtic Druidism spoke so powerfully to me. It reveres and seeks divine guidance in both the Goddess and God. They are both equal parts of Oneness.

The form of Celtic Druidism I learned is a Welsh tradition known as "Gwyddonic Druidism." Officially instituted in the 1600s, the Gwyddonic Order was created to preserve a religion and philosophy that is thousands of years old. This ancient tradition provides a pathway to your true nature; its philosophical foundation being that all things are One, whatsoever they may be.

From the well-documented works of authors Jean Markale and Zecharia Sitchin, as well as from the Celtic oral tradition itself and volumes of folklore and historical references, it is very probable that the mysterious Anunnaki are related to aspects of Druidism. Written on the ancient Sumerian clay tablets and recorded in ancient Babylonian mythology, the Anunnaki were the children or followers of An (Anu, Ana), and also the stars or Sky-Gods that came down to the Earth. An was the Sky-God and creator of the star spirits of the great Sumerian triad of Anu, Enlil, and Ea. The Sumerian Male Anu parallels the female Tuatha De

Danann Anu, Ana, and Danu. In Druidism, Anu is considered the Mother of the Gods, from whom all other Gods stem. Interestingly, during Gwyddonic ritual I have always heard her called "Anu," not Danu.

Bel (Beli) is the first-born son (sun) of Anu of the Tuatha De Danann, and parallels the great Mesopotamian God Bel. The word Danann is often shown as D'Annan, meaning "of An," again linking the Sky-God An together with the Tuatha Goddess Anu. Keep in mind that both masculine and feminine characteristics were ascribed to the ancient Gods. Both Goddesses and Gods were solar, lunar, stellar, and planetary, and often had a combination of these aspects.

The Gwyddonic Druid tradition represents pieces of the ancient knowledge of the Sky-Gods that came down to Earth, combined with a mixture of ancient aboriginal faiths of the native peoples of the northern parts of Great Britain, including the influences of the Hyperboreans, Tuatha De Danann, Prytani, and later the Celts.

The word *Gwyddonaid* in archaic entries means "wizard" or "tree witch." *Gwyddon* is Welsh for "wise one." The Gwyddonaid consists of the philosophy of the "Old Tribes" or the "Old Religion" of Northern Europe, combined with the mystical teachings and wisdom of the powerful Prytanes of Greece, and the lore and traditions of the conquering Celtic peoples that swept through the British Isles. Within this context, Gwyddonic Druidism is a kind of spiritual stew that has gathered its wisdom from many different peoples. A testament to the basic Druid philosophy of Oneness, the "Old Tribal Bards" existed well into the middle of the 18th century. Today Druidism, like many Earth-spirited traditions, is experiencing a tremendous renaissance.

The Gwyddonic Druid tradition places emphasis on the astronomical observances of the sun and moon, with particular emphasis on the sun. The Gwyddonic Druid New Year begins on Yule, when the sun grows stronger. The "new" Gwyddonic Druid Calendar begins on the Winter Solstice, 1900 B.C.E., at the waning of the Age of Taurus and the dawning of the Age of Aries. This is also the date the finishing touches were completed on Stonehenge, and also when the Tuatha De Danann disappeared into a mystical dream world or Otherworld, where they became heroes and deities.

Five Noble Families held and protected the ancient teachings of the Druids and the Gwyddonaid. During the Renaissance, the Gwyddonaid are said to have awakened from their long slumber, and around 1650 C.E., the *Greater Book of the Art and Craft* was written down for the first time in Welsh.

The first Gwyddonic Druid College was founded by a lady of noble birth, High Priestess MEM, in London, England, in the late 1700s. Corvin was her High Priest, and he brought the Gwyddonaid teachings to the New World in 1792. Corvin settled in Salem, Massachusetts, and passed the knowledge on to Cordemanon Lughkin. Lughkin moved to Baltimore, Maryland, and he entrusted the teachings to Anna Ravenwood prior to his death in 1899. Anna moved to San Francisco, California, and in 1947 translated the *Greater Book of the Art and Craft* from the native Welsh into English. Anna spread the teachings of the Gwyddonaid to several students in the San Francisco Bay Area and in Sacramento, California, where she eventually settled and was active in the craft until her death in the early 1970s. My teacher, the Fox, met Anna in 1954, and was her student and Priest.

Cordemanon is the title of those who carry on the wisdom of the Gwyddonic tradition. The word *Cordemanon* means "the mouthpiece of the Gods" or "caretaker of the sacred knowledge." Divinely entrusted, Cordemanons are individuals who have incarnated with the specific intention of sharing the wisdom and practices of the Gwyddonaid with others. All of us are like children awakening and arising, ready to build the Great Pattern, a pattern that the Cordemanons designed a long time ago.

The practices and wisdom of the Gwyddonic Druid tradition embody a synthesis of cultures and spiritual philosophies, passed down through generations, while continually being influenced and updated. Gwyddonic Druidism is an evolution of pagan concepts and practices. It is a spiritual practice without all the dogma of most religions. For me, this was the greatest appeal of the tradition.

The Gwyddonic Druid tradition is closely related to the Welsh rite Gwyddonaid, which is a Welsh/Celtic tradition of Wicca that works with the Welsh Pantheon of Gods and Goddesses. The Welsh Gwyddonaid means "Tree Witch." Within the Welsh rite Gwyddonaid, the eight Sabbats and 13 full moons are observed. Many elements of the Gwyddonaid rituals continue to be practiced in folk traditions in Wales today.

The purpose of this book is to take you on a journey through the teachings as they were taught to me and to share my experiences. I found Gwyddonic Druid training to be useful as a jumping-off point for learning the old ways, but since then I've had a chance to update the teachings so they work on a practical level, particularly within the context of modern society.

As I continually point out in this book, Celtic Druidism is a living tradition that continues to change and adapt to people's needs. This is what originally drew me to it in the first place and now continues to propel me forward in my spiritual quest. After reading this book, I hope Celtic Druidism will also empower you on your personal quest. Blessed be!

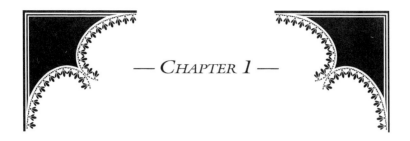

CHAPTER 1

THE DRUIDS

The Druids and the Standing Stones

There are more than 1,300 stone circles in Britain, Ireland, and Brittany. Even though the origin of these stone monuments is debatable, the group of people most often associated with them is the Druids. Stonehenge stands out as the stone circle most closely tied to the Druids. It is there that the Druids hold their Midsummer's Eve Rituals. John Aubrey, a 17th-century British historian, went so far as to say that the Druids were the ones who built Stonehenge. This theory has never been actually proven or disproved. The origin of the Druids and the people who built Stonehenge both remain mysteries. As with most mysteries, there are clues, but no conclusive answers. Janet and Colin Bord, in their book *Mysterious Britain* write, "The best-known prehistoric monument in Britain is associated in many people's minds with Druids, but Stonehenge is probably older than Druidism—though this itself is a vague name for a teaching that has existed for untold millennia."

Stonehenge

Like the pyramids of Egypt, Stonehenge stands as a marvel of ancient craftsmanship. Built in three stages from 3100 to 1100 B.C.E., it consists of a circle of massive stones with a "heel stone," which is almost 20 feet high and weighs about 70,000 pounds. Stonehenge also has a set of five Saracenic stones, weighing up to 90,000 pounds, which have a third stone, known as a lintel stone, laid across their top. One of the wonders is that each of the cross stones has been expertly carved on each side so that they fit tongue and groove into the upright Saracenic stones. Even today, this would take incredible skill, but in terms of what we expect from supposedly primitive people, Stonehenge represents a miraculous achievement that has survived the ages.

Because the standing stones at Stonehenge are so large and well put together, they have given rise to many theories, including ones that report that the massive stones came from distant places by magickal means. Geoffrey of Monmouth, a 12th-century English writer noted for his Arthurian tales, wrote that Merlin the Magician magickally transported the gigantic stones to their resting place. At the bidding of the king, Merlin moved the stones several hundred miles, from Ireland, where they were called the "Giants Dance," to the Salisbury Plain in England, where they stand today.

Regarding the mystery as to who created Stonehenge, recent archeological evidence dates Stonehenge back four to six thousand years. The Celts are reported to not have arrived in Britain until about 900 to 700 B.C.E, which is a thousand or more years later than the building of Stonehenge. Jean Markale, historian and author of *The Druids: Celtic Priests of Nature*, paints a larger perspective when he says:

> If folk tradition has linked Druidism to the megaliths,
> it is perhaps because there is a certain rapport between

them, even if vague or secondary in nature. After all, the Irish mythological texts make the megalithic mounds into the dwellings of the ancient Gods; this placement cannot be due to chance, and assuredly poses a problem that cannot be avoided by seeking refuge behind archaeological convictions.

Historically, it was common for the conquering peoples to move in and take over the temples and shrines of the people they conquered. For example, many of the sacred Irish pagan sites were used as places to build Christian churches and cathedrals. Even if the Druids did not build monoliths such as Stonehenge, they definitely made use of what was there, to the extent that it became part of the mythology surrounding both the standing stones and the Druids.

The Druids considered the standing stones, also known as the "speaking stones" or "whisperers," to be alive. This is why they would pilgrimage to Stonehenge on the Summer Solstice, the longest day of year. They felt the standing stones represented a living vortex into other worlds.

The Druids kept track of the cycles of the sun and moon. The Great Days and festivals are based on certain solar and lunar calculations. For example, the May festival of Beltane is calculated halfway between the Spring Equinox and Summer Solstice, just as the Druid festival of Samhain, which is known today as Halloween, is calculated halfway between the Fall Equinox and the Winter Solstice.

Another interesting thing about the standing stones is that many, if not all of them, are tied to the paths of the sun and moon. Stonehenge, called "Temple of Apollo" by early Greek and Roman writers, was an early observatory. The huge standing stones are positioned in such a way as to mark the paths of the sun and moon.

The astrological significance surrounding Stonehenge was reported by Roman author Diodorus Siculus, who wrote that the Sun God returned to the site every 19 years. There are 18 years and seven months in a lunar node cycle, where the moon crosses the path of the sun, and which Stonehenge accurately marks.

Professor Gerald Hawkins of Boston University, in his book *Stonehenge Decoded*, asserts that 10 of the stones in the circle record positions of the sun within one degree, and another 14 stones point to extreme positions of the moon. Besides the axis, which points to Midsummer's sunrise, two of the other stones are believed to mark the Druid festivals of Beltane and Samhain.

Along with Stonehenge, other ancient observatories used by the Druids are Carnac in Brittany, where 3,000 stones stand grouped in a five-mile area, and Newgrange, located in the Boyne River Valley in Ireland, where the stones line up with the rising sun at the Winter Solstice. This is the time of the Celtic Druid Winter festival of Yule. Because of the vast numbers of standing stones throughout the Celtic lands, and because the stones often mark the paths of sun and moon, it is easy to see why the Druids used the stones even if they themselves didn't put them there.

The alignment of the stones is not coincidental. They are based on the paths of sun and moon, much like the teachings of modern Druids. Although the origins of the standing stones and Druidism are shrouded in mystery, both have withstood the ages, a testament to an ancient and powerful knowledge. We are only now beginning to understand the extent of this knowledge from a culture that we have historically viewed as primitive. As with the standing stones, the mystery of the Druids is equally perplexing, as they had a highly evolved spirituality even by today's standards.

Who Were the Druids?

Druidism is Britain's oldest religion. No one knows where the Druids originated, but all agree that they stem from the ancient tribes of Europe. Some say that the Druids migrated to the West from the Altai region in Siberia, a place known for its shamans. Still others say that the Druids were the descendants of Abraham of the Israelites, or that they came from Tibet, Egypt, or Babylonia, and were part of the Cult of the Dead.

Many of the early tribal cultures had a name for their magickal priests and priestesses. "Druid" is one of those many names; it is a name associated with Celts more than any other culture. The Greeks first recorded the word *Druidae*. The word *Druid* is akin to the Greek *drus* (*drys*, *dhrys*) meaning "an oak." Some scholars suggest that the word *Druid* stems from "derw," the Old Celtic name for oak. Others say "dru-wid" or "dru-vid" means "oak knowledge," with "wid" or "vid" meaning "to know." Still others say the word *Druid* comes from the British "dar," meaning "superior," or "Gwydd," meaning "wise one." In Scottish Gaelic, "Druidh" means "magician."

In an Irish story, the God Lugh first approaches Tara, the home of the Gods and Goddesses, and is asked, "What is your profession?" One after another, he lists his many skills including carpenter, smith, harpist, magician, and so forth. Each time he lists another profession, the doorman says that there is already a God present who excels at that craft. Finally Lugh says, "Then ask the king if he has with him a man who is master of these crafts at once because if he does, there is no need for me to come to Tara." After beating the king's champion at a game of chess, Lugh is admitted into the halls of the Gods as the "master of all arts and crafts."

In terms of the Druids, this story exemplifies how they viewed themselves: the masters of all arts and crafts. As such, their teachings often took many years to learn. Druidism was primarily an oral tradition that stressed the student's ability to memorize its teachings. Because it started as an oral tradition, Druidism has from the outset been a living tradition and thereby in a continual state of transformation. This concept of a living tradition moving forward through time, and in the process evolving, is in step with the spiritual teachings of the ancient Druids, who believed that we all move between this world and the Otherworld. With each transition, we move closer to a divine state of being of Godhood and Goddesshood.

The Druids followed the path of the sun. It makes sense that the first scientific and spiritual connection humans would make would be with the path of the sun. The standing stones, the Druids, and the Celts were all highly tied into the cycles of the sun, as evidenced by seasonal festivals that occur at particular astronomical times.

Like the *Farmer's Almanac* of their day, the Druids had their own methods for calculating when to plant crops and when to hold the spiritual celebrations. Rather than competing with or controlling nature, the Druids lived and connected with her many cycles. They celebrated each season as an extension of the Goddess and God.

Understanding the cycles and progressions of life was essential to the teachings of the Druids. Whether caterpillar, cocoon, or butterfly, the progression is always one in which life moves forward in cycles. The Earth and its relation to the sun moves through four stages—Summer, Winter, Spring, and Fall. These stages are essential to the cycle of life and rebirth. The Druids understood this simple concept, and based much of their teachings on these natural cycles. They knew that all living things are affected by the progressions of the seasons.

Because of their basic similarities, many historians have suggested Druidism and Hinduism have a common source. Recent evidence suggests that both Druidism and Hinduism evolved separately from common Indo-European roots. Both are also pantheistic spiritual philosophies that believe in basic reincarnation, something not traditionally accepted in the Mediterranean World.

Another region to which Druidism has been traditionally linked is the Mediterranean, and the cultures of Egypt, Greece, and Rome. In his book *The Druids*, Jean Markale states:

> Druidism did not originate in the Mediterranean region. If it had, the Greeks and Romans would not have failed to say so. It is true that they generally revealed themselves as stupefied to observe the grandeur and eminence of a doctrine that did not belong to their world, and which, therefore, they classified, for lack of a better word, as "barbarian." This term essentially designated the inhabitants of Europe who had not yet been ranked under Roman domination, and who had not been touched by Greek civilization. One is forced to recognize a certain Nordic character of this population (or group of populations), who were feared by the Greeks, but who also fired their imaginations.

The Norse connection with the Celtic Druids is definitely pronounced. They both saw themselves as descended from a race of giants. The first people were the Gods and Goddesses, and the Norse "vitki" or rune-masters, like the Celtic Druids did, invoked these ancient Goddess and God energies when doing magick.

The Celtic-Norse connection is a significant one. When I was first learning Celtic Druidism, my teacher gave me a copy of the poem "The Lay of the High One," which is a key piece in Norse mythology from the *Elder Edda*. Also known as "Odin's Magickal Songs," the poem I received read:

> For all of nine stormy nights
> I hung upon the tree,
> Wounded by my own blade
> Odin consecrated to Odin
> An offering of myself to myself;
> Bound to that mighty tree
> Whose roots men know not!
> None gave me to eat
> None gave me to drink,
> Down into the abyss I wandered
> And sought out the runes!
> Then I fell into the darkness with a great cry!
> Rebirth I attained
> And also wisdom
> For I grew strong and exalted in my growing;
> Thus from one rune was I led to a second
> From one act to another.

This poem describes a shamanic experience that is akin to the Druid concept of merging. When you merge, you become one with the totality of the universe. Merging is a key ingredient to magick. In a modern sense, merging can be compared to a heightened sense of focus that takes on divine proportions. With the right focus, you can attain your goals.

The Druids had an evolved spiritual connection to the Earth, including her cycles and her numerous inhabitants— animal, vegetable, and mineral. No doubt, beginning with hunter and gatherer societies, the spirituality and teachings of the Druids evolved into an agricultural and herding-based philosophy. As it evolved, Celtic society continued to derive much of its means of support from the connection with nature. Farming and herding relied on both a practical and spiritual knowledge of the cycles of the Earth, sun, and moon.

Through time, the land has become a treasure trove of ancestral power. It is like a repository of ancestral knowledge, with the ancient sleepers just waiting to be awakened. Modern Druids suggest ways you can tap into the power of the land and become one with an energy as ancient as all of creation.

Although like the standing stones, no one knows where the Druids originated, the dust is beginning to settle. Most everyone agrees that the Druids existed throughout the Celtic world, in one form or another. They were found in Ireland, Britain, and throughout Gaul (mainland Europe), including Spain, Italy, Galatia, the Danube Valley, and other adjacent areas. At one time, their sphere of influence included the area from the British Isles to Turkey.

Who Were the Celts?

From a paradise located in the Danube Valley, the Indo-European tribes migrated outward, spreading their culture, language, and spirituality. They migrated East to Asia, South to the Mediterranean Sea, North to Scandinavia, and West to the Celtic lands. All these tribes carried their seeds throughout the world, which is why so many cultures seem so similar, even such diverse groups as the Indian Hindus and the Western European Celts.

From the headwaters of the Danube, the Celts migrated across the vast expanses of northwestern Europe. The Celts and the other Germanic tribes moved out of the Danube in waves to Scotland, Ireland, England, Wales, and Brittany (France). Culturally, linguistically, and spiritually the Celts were more tied to the Norse and Germanic traditions than to the Mediterranean and Eastern cultures. It's like an extended family where everyone is related, but some connections are more pronounced than others.

The Celtic connection to the Danube River Valley is expressed in their original name, "The Children of Danu." The children of Danu, whose Irish name is the "Tuatha De Danann," invaded on Beltane (May Day) in a mist that hid their advance. They were most likely the fabled Hyperboreans who dwelt on the islands at the northernmost reaches of the world. The Hyperboreans were known to practice Druidism, sorcery, shapeshifting, and astronomy. They conquered and ruled over Ireland for many years, and eventually they were conquered, again by an army that arrived on Beltane. The Tuatha migrated into the hills and mounds of Ireland after they were conquered. In doing this, they became the Celtic Goddesses and Gods, divinely connected to the Earth.

Danu is an ancient and original Mother Goddess. She was brought to Europe and Asia by the migrating Indo-European tribes. Also known as Dana, Ann, and Anu, the spiritual tradition of Danu is one of the oldest traditions. In general, the concept of the Mother Goddess, whose many aspects are tied to the cycles of the Earth, is at the source of many ancient European spiritual traditions. Peter Ellis, in his book *The Druids*, writes:

> Like most world religions, the Celts started with a 'Mother Goddess' concept. In the case of the Celts, the Mother Goddess was Danu ('water from heaven') and it is significant that the great river Danube takes its name from her; significant, that is, because it was at the headwaters of the Danube that Celtic civilization is acknowledged to have evolved.

With the many different invaders that swept across Europe, the Celtic world was conquered and influenced by consecutive waves of Indo-European cultures. The mythological history of Ireland speaks of five invasions. The first was the race of Partholon, whose leader came from the Otherworld. Partholon invaded on Beltane and ruled Ireland for 300 years, in which time the island increased in size from one plain to four and added seven new lakes. The second wave of invaders was the race of Nemed, who carried on the work and traditions of the Partholon. The Nemed fought with the Fomors, who in some legends are giants. Initially the Nemed were successful in their struggle. Later they were struck down by an epidemic. Some historians maintain that the Nemed and Partholon are one and the same and actually describe a single invading wave of people.

The Fir Bolgs, or "men of Bolgs" represent the third wave of invaders that swept through Ireland. They were three tribes who divided Ireland among them, with the Fir Gaillion in Leinster, the Fir Domnann in Munster and Connaught, and the Fir Bolg in Ulster. As a race, the Fir Bolgs were reported to be "dark Iberians," who practiced strange magickal rites in their inaccessible forts among the hills and mountains.

The next invading force was that of the Tuatha De Danann, who as I described earlier, arrived in a mist on Beltane. Early legend says the Tuatha came from the sky and brought with them four gifts: Nuada's Sword; Lugh's Terrible Lance; Dagda's Cauldron; and the Stone of Fal, or "Stone of Destiny." Legend says the Druid priests of the Fir Bolgs waged war against the Druid priests of the Tuatha De Danann until at last, in a battle started on Midsummer, "The Children of Danu" were victorious in their conquest of Ireland.

The "Sons of Mil," the last wave of invaders, are the mythological equivalent to modern humans. At the point that humans became supreme, the forces of the Tuatha De Danann went underground and became part of the land, an energy that is waiting to be tapped into and utilized. The Goddesses and Gods did not die, but became part of the whole of

Oneness, representing a knowledge that is like an energetic library, waiting for us to tap into it and utilize its infinite database.

The power of knowledge is an infinite power, and Oneness is the boundless source. Each wave of invaders brought their own ideas, which then intermingled with ideas of the people who were already living there. This exchange of ideas produced a synthesis that continued with each invading population. This is why some of the main religions of the world have become melting pots for the spiritual traditions that preceded them.

Documented evidence suggests that the major body of Celts did not arrive in Britain until 900 to 700 B.C.E., but at the same time the Celts were culturally related, and adapted some of the social and spiritual customs of the people before them. In one form or another, Celtic Druidism evolved over a period of time, changing each time it came into contact with other cultures. This was especially true when the Celts migrated into Western Europe.

Before the Roman invasion, the Druids and their beliefs and practices flourished in Celtic society. Later Celtic history and spirituality were influenced first by the Romans, then the Christians, who both obviously had their own agendas. The Romans and Christians systematically exterminated the Druids, who they regarded as a real threat. They rationalized their brutality by reporting that the Celts were practicing human sacrifice. In the Druid tradition I was taught, it is forbidden to kill another person or "give dead things to the Lady." The Celts embraced life, which is why their spirituality is rooted in the cycles of the nature. They worshipped the living "Mother Goddess."

After trying to exterminate Celtic Druidism, the Christians then went on to adopt as much Celtic lore as possible.

Many of the Goddesses and Gods of the Tuatha De Danann became saints. For example, the Celtic Goddess Bridget became Saint Bridget. The Celtic Festival of Yule, celebrating the birth of the sun at the Winter Solstice, became the birthday of Christ, the Son of God and of light.

In the Gwyddonic Druid tradition, the teachings say that "Before the coming of the Sky-Gods, she [the Goddess] was the Sun and Moon, but now they say she is only the Moon. But to us she is still all things."

Unfortunately, the only history that has survived was written down by the Romans and then the Christians. Their views were tainted as they wanted to justify their acts of barbarism against the Celts, much like the white man justified eliminating the Native Americans and Australian Aborigines. By making the Celts less than human, they justified the extermination of the Celtic culture, and in doing so, destroyed much practical spiritual wisdom.

First the Romans, and then the Christians, outlawed Celtic Druidism to the point where anyone caught practicing the "Old Religion" was put to death. Even these extreme punishments did not stop the Druids, but they did drive them further underground. Still today, there is an air of secrecy and mystery surrounding the teachings and rituals of Celtic Druidism.

Modern Celtic Druidism

The spiritual tradition of the Goddess is at the roots of humanity. This is one of the reasons people have an innate connection to Druidism. All living things join together in the cycles of birth, life, death, and rebirth. Understanding and utilizing these cycles is what Celtic Druidism is all about.

On some level, it's what spirituality is about—our connection to the boundless whole, which we as people see as divine.

Rather than resurrecting the ancient Druid teachings and keeping them the way they were, modern Celtic Druidism is about evolving these ideas into the 21st century. What these ancient teachings give is a platform for connecting with nature in a more positive way. Also, early Druidism was based on the Goddess or Divine Mother. Only later did it become more paternal and God-oriented. This was due to outside influences, particularly that of the Romans and early Christians, who were both very male-dominated societies and were threatened by the equal status women were given in Celtic society.

Modern Druidism is about integrating both female and male energies, instead of just focusing one or the other. Because of this, Druid practices use all divine energies, meaning it includes all forms of energy and excludes none. You can believe in any Gods, many Gods, one Goddess, two, three, 10, or none, and still be a Druid. There are no rules.

A Druid uses the power of the land, cycles of energy, and the power of the mind to direct energy to intended goals. A power resides within the land that waits to be released for your benefit. The land can empower you or the land can take you down depending on your relationship to it. Cut down all her trees and desecrate the Mother's Earthly body, and in turn she will make sure your goals and aspirations never come to fruition. Work with her and connect to the power of the land, and anything is possible. Plant the seed, cultivate and water it, and it will grow into wondrous things.

Many 20th-century writers, such as Ernest Hemingway, wrote about the struggle of "man against nature," ignorantly suggesting that nature was something to be controlled and ruled over. This attitude is apparent in large cities, where nature has been paved over and beaten into submission by bulldozers, concrete, and asphalt. There is inherently nothing wrong with the concept of cities; it comes down to our attitudes as people toward nature. Again it's a struggle of "us and them," as if somehow you can separate people from nature. We forget we are part of nature and the Earth. If we kill the Earth, we kill ourselves. It's that simple.

Our task as modern Druids is to live with and learn from nature. Nature is our friend, not our enemy. If we help sustain nature, it will help sustain us. By becoming One with nature, we release our innate power. We connect to the infiniteness of being, making us whole again. Technology is wonderful, but we need to use it in accordance with nature, rather than as a means for controlling her.

Celtic Druidism is a spiritual tradition that finds its roots in the Earth and in the honoring of ancestors. The center of Druidism is the quest for inspiration or Awen, meaning "the flowing breath of the spirit." In the United States, there are hundreds of Druid groups. In England, more than 50 recognized groups practice various forms of modern Celtic Druidism. This includes people from other faiths, ranging from Catholics to Jews, who incorporate their faith into the Druid tradition. People who practice Druidism come from a wide range of backgrounds, blue collar to white collar, from teachers, office workers, corporate leaders, and store owners, to artisans, actors, musicians, and modern magicians. All this diversity is made possible by the fact that the Druid tradition accepts everyone.

The Concept of Oneness

Oneness is an essential concept in Celtic Druidism. It is the concept that connects everything into the whole of existence. Within Oneness are the divine energies of all the Goddesses and Gods. Everything is included and a part of Oneness.

Many cultures and traditions share the concept of Oneness. Plato described the cosmos as fashioned into a single visible creature containing within itself all living things whose nature is of the same order. Native American tradition states that in the beginning was Wakan, and Wakan is the great void. She is the great circle. She is everything. The East Indian philosophy of Kashmir Shaivism adheres to the belief that all things spring out of nothingness, and the spark of energy is within the whole universe and all its individual parts, meaning it is all interconnected and the same. Zen Buddhist philosophy says that before we were born we had no feeling; we were one with the universe. After we are separated by birth from this oneness, as the water falling from the waterfall is separated by the wind and rocks, then we have feeling. When you do not realize that you are one with the river, or one with the universe, you have fear.

We are all connected together by an etheric force that is both minute and infinite. Oneness is like a giant, boundless web that connects all things together into a whole. From the One comes the whole of existence, and from the whole comes each individual part of Oneness. We are all part of Oneness. Oneness is One boundless being, so there is a part of us that is also boundless.

Modern physics explains that everything came from a common point, which, when it exploded, became the big bang, creating the infiniteness of the universe. The Concept of Oneness comes from the idea that all this infiniteness creates a cohesion of energy that connects everything together. This connection is called Oneness. It's all-inclusive; hot-cold, female-male, and good-bad. Everything, no matter what energy state, form, color, density, duration, and so forth, is part of Oneness. Each aspect of Oneness is truly unique, yet each aspect is also fully the One and part of the commonality. Every aspect of the One can never be more or less of the One. Everything revolves around the polarities, and at some point the polarities converge into Oneness. Divinity is female and male, integrating both into a whole. This whole is the divine face of Oneness.

Oneness is the energetic connection between all that has been, is, and will ever be. When you imagine everything as Oneness, you begin to understand the connections between things rather than the separations. Each piece comes together, linked into a fabric that is tightly woven together into a whole. One piece of the puzzle effects every other piece and vice versa.

As humans, each cell joins with other cells to make up the whole of our body. If a disease such as cancer effects a single cell, then it is felt by the whole of our body. In return, what we eat and put into our bodies as a whole, affects every individual cell. This also includes the thoughts we think and our spiritual attitudes toward life itself. Everything we allow into our being, into our energetic field, influences us in ways that can only be measured through time.

Merging with Oneness

Tapping into Oneness is a way for people to stay connected to their bodies as well as to the natural cycles of the Earth. In modern Celtic Druidism this tapping into Oneness is a process called merging, which involves diffusing your personal energy outward like a cloud. Through merging, you can experience an awareness of Oneness. By doing so, you realize that Oneness is the true state of existence. You can then apply this knowledge to practical advantage.

You can use deep breathing for merging. For example, count to three as you take a deep breath, then hold your breath for three seconds, and then exhale to the count of three—a total of nine seconds for each deep breath you take. Exhale completely while imagining your breath and energy move into Oneness with the divine. When merging, there is a change in perception as the boundaries and separation of this world and other realms become less distinct and more fluid. With practice, you can move at will to Otherworlds by merging and intending on being there.

The following is an exercise that can help you to begin merging. I use a tree as a jumping-off point, but once you have gone through the exercise a few times, you can use anything you want. By becoming the things around you, you begin merging and becoming One with the divine energy of the Goddess and God. If you have trouble doing this exercise, just pretend to do it at first. Pretending sometimes helps get you into a mind-set for experiencing new things.

When first doing this exercise, it helps to have a tree in front of you as a point of reference. As you recite each line, take time to become that aspect before moving to the next line. The idea with this exercise is to shift you into a merged state of consciousness. Look at the tree, and repeat aloud:

> I am the tree, the tree is me,
> I am the roots, the roots are me,
> I am the trunk, the trunk is me,
> I am the bark, the bark is me,
> I am the branches, the branches are me,
> I am the leaves, the leaves are me,
> I am the bird in the tree, the bird in the tree is me,
> I am the sky, the sky is me,
> I am the air, the air is me,
> I am the clouds, the clouds are me,

I am the water, the water is me,
I am the fire of life, the fire of life is me,
I am the Earth, the Earth is me,
I am all things, and all things are me,
I am Oneness, and Oneness is me.
We are One. Blessed be!

With the last line, feel your energy move and diffuse into everything around you. Feel your energy shift and expand. Continue doing this exercise until merging comes naturally. You will feel more centered when your are merging and your mind is turned toward the Concept of Oneness.

Thresholds to Otherworlds and Dimensions

Time is speculative. It can be seen as a movement of energy across the vast expanse of Oneness. As humans we are linear beings and have a tendency to think in linear terms. Yet the universe is not by any means linear. Quite the opposite. The universe has a stirring motion to it, meaning that at some point polarities come together as One. Called "the razor's edge" in modern mythology, this is the place where points, polarities, and worlds converge, where there is no distinction or separation. This is the threshold to Otherworlds and dimensions. Shamans, priestesses, and priests all go to this place to connect with the divine.

In Celtic mythology, there are many stories about Otherworlds, with many heroic tales taking place in these kingdoms. Tirfo Thuinn is the Land under the Waves, still occasionally seen today. The Land of the Young, Tir-nan-Og, also called the Land of Beauty and home to the Tuatha De Danann, lies west across the sea. It is a paradise where there is no time or death, and a place where the grass is green and fruit and flowers bloom. Another Celtic Otherworld of sunshine and rest is called the Isle of the Blest "Hy-Brasail."

The Celts were ancestor worshippers, and their deities were also the ancestors of the clan. Many stories and legends center around the explanation of how these ancestors made perilous journeys into the Otherworld realms in order to perform a task or undergo some sort of transformation.

You need not travel great distances to visit the Otherworld. It's everywhere, and its location can be accessed depending upon the relative location of your awareness. In other words, the Otherworld is ever-present. It's just that your attention is here, not there in the Otherworld.

During certain times of the year, generally on the Eight Great Days and full moons, the threshold to the Otherworlds of experience are flung open. This is an optimum time to do rituals and magical works. Magick provides a doorway to enter these thresholds and experience the varying dimensions of time and space.

The Nematon

Ancient Druids worshipped in forests under the trees. Before the Roman Conquest, the Celts never erected temples. They felt that communion with the divine was only possible in the woods or in areas away from other people. The very land itself held spiritual significance. These natural, sacred areas were called "nematons." The Druids held religious ceremonies in these nematons.

The word *nematon* means a circular clearing in the woods and mystical sanctuary. Seen as an opening between worlds where divine and earthly meet, usually the nematon is found in a forest grove consisting of oaks, ash, rowan, and birch trees. Sometimes a creek or spring flows next to the nematon. The water symbolizes a link to the subterranean Otherworld.

The natural grove of trees of the nematon attracts the spirits of the Sky-World or Otherworld to the mortal world. The nematon is the home of the thunder and lightning Sky-God, and also the tree spirits called dryads.

The modern Celtic Druid's nematon can consist of a staff that stands upright in the center of the area that is called "the bill." At the South is the fire pit (or holder) and to the North a cauldron, or well of water. Usually a hole or shaft is dug next to the well to receive offerings. These offerings are the sacred meal of the Mother. Traditionally, they are silver for the well, oil for the fire, honey, red wine, apples, bread, salt, and ale.

Your personal nematon can be situated wherever you choose. Its purpose is to act as a threshold to Otherworlds of experience. For example, you can select a favorite place in nature as your nematon. Just sitting in your garden listening to the sound of the wind can transport you to Otherworlds. Sitting under a tree, watching its shadow move upon the ground as the breeze softly moves through its branches can take you through the threshold. Watching the water flow in a waterfall, fountain, creek, or ocean, until everything seems to alter around you can transport you into an Otherworldly experience. Playing a musical instrument, singing, and chanting can also take you there.

Dreaming is perhaps the easiest way to reach the Otherworld. Just before going to sleep and just upon waking in the morning, give yourself the suggestion, over and over, that you will have a most pleasant visit to the Celtic Otherworld in your dreams, and that you will remember your experience when you wake up. Do this every night until you remember a dream about visiting a Celtic Otherworld. Most people get positive results within a week. I also suggest you write down your Otherworldly dreams into your notebook or dream journal for later reference.

The Elements of Power

The four Elements of power are Earth, Air, Fire, and Water. They flow from Oneness. Familiarizing yourself with each of these Elements and their qualities is an essential part of Celtic Druidism. Even the Great Circle corresponds to the Elements of power and the four directions of North, East, South, and West.

The Element of the North point is Earth, symbolized on the altar by a bowl of salt or soil. The Earth element has a grounding and stabilizing effect. In astrology, this Element is represented in the signs Taurus, Virgo, and Capricorn, whose main traits are dependability, endurance, stubbornness, and practicality. Mastery of the Earth element involves being connected to the structure, strength, and practical nature of things.

The East point corresponds to the Air element, represented on the altar by the incense and censer. The element of Air has the ability to move through just about anything. In astrology, this Element is represented in the signs of Gemini, Libra, and Aquarius, whose main traits are sociability, perception, communication, and intellectual ability. Mastery of the Air element involves being detached from things and the ability to move around or through anything. Just as Earth is structured, Air is very unstructured.

The South point represents the Fire element. It is represented on the altar by the burning candle and candlestick. Fire is the Element of action, noted by the expression "all fired up," meaning ready to go. The astrological signs associated with the element of Fire are Aries, Leo, and Sagittarius, whose main traits are expansion, personal drive, and the ability to have a lot of energy and burn brightly. Mastery of the Fire element gives you immense transformative power and creative ability.

The West point corresponds to the Water element, symbolized on the altar by the chalice of water. Water has the ability to move and flow much like energy flows. Water signs are Cancer, Scorpio, and Pisces, whose main traits are intuition, emotion, wisdom, and secrecy. Mastery of the Water element gives you the ability to use the flow of energy to attain your goals and to be very fruitful in your endeavors.

Enhance your connection with the elements by associating them with different areas of your being. Chant these words aloud:

> My flesh and bones are the earth.
> The earth is my flesh and bones.
> We are One.
> My breath is the air.
> The air is my breath.
> We are One.
> My eyes are the light.
> The light is my eyes.
> We are One.
> My emotions are water.
> Water is my emotions.
> We are One.
> I am all elements.
> All elements are me.
> We are One.

Four Treasures Meditation

The Tuatha De Danann brought four treasures with them to Ireland that are connected to the Elements of power. The Stone of Fal or Stone of Destiny is connected to the Earth element, and has the qualities of wisdom, virtue, and destiny. The element of Air connects to Nuada's Sword, whose qualities are truth and discrimination. Lugh's Terrible Lance or spear is the treasure associated with the Fire element and has the qualities of victory and knowing the path or the way. (Lugh's lance is considered terrible because it was alive and thirsted for blood so much so that it could be kept at rest only by putting its head in a bath of pounded poppy leaves. It roared in battle and fire flashed from it as it tore through the ranks of the enemies.) Dagda's Cauldron is associated with the Water element. It is inexhaustible and has the qualities of wealth and abundance.

The following meditation uses the four treasures and their corresponding Element to help you better understand the Elements of power. I suggest you read it over a couple times, and then try it, or tape record it, and play it back.

Begin by getting comfortable. Loosen any clothing that might be binding you. Take off your shoes, and sit or recline. Close your eyes and breathe deeply, inhaling and exhaling slowly, feeling more relaxed each time you let your breath out. Imagine the tension and stress evaporating from your body as you become more and more relaxed. Feel yourself melt into the surface that you are sitting or laying on as you breathe deeply and completely.

Without the burden of your worries and responsibilities, imagine yourself beginning to float upward to the ceiling. Once you reach the ceiling, you realize you're flying, and you begin moving like you're swimming through air. Moving your arms, you float out of the room, and once outside you rise upward like a firefly on a warm summer's eve. Up through the branches of the trees you float until eventually you are above treetops, looking down on the world below.

After floating for a while, you descend slowly downward. Like a leaf on a gentle breeze, you gradually drop down into the center of a stone circle. The stones that dot the perimeter of the circle are massive, each casting a giant shadow that converge upon the center.

You move to the North point or the circle, marked by a stone of considerable size. As you touch this stone, you see a bluish light glowing from the stone into your hand, and you can feel its power moving from the ground upward into your body. In an instant, you see your past, present, and future. The patterns of your life unfold before you, and the faces of your ancestors flash before you.

Next you move to the East point, marked by a sword laying on a white quartz stone altar of gigantic proportions. As you take the handle of the sword in your hand, you feel invincible. Everything is yours for the asking and anything is possible. Laying the sword back down upon the white stone altar, you feel an inner vision awakening within you like a strong wind blowing. You sense an eye of truth appearing in the center of your forehead, and suddenly your vision is greatly expanded.

Moving to the South point of the circle, you see a spear mounted on a monolith. As you touch the spear, you know and understand that your positive patterns and ventures will be successful. You feel a fire that burns in your inner core that sustains the light of your life. Your body feels as though it were on fire as you hold the mighty spear. Sense the light within yourself burning brighter.

As you move toward the West point, you see a giant stone pillar with a cauldron in front of it. From the cauldron springs ultimate abundance so that you want for nothing. As you spread its water on your body with your fingertips, soon every part is healed of any disease. You feel healthier and more alive and refreshed than you have ever felt. Feel yourself merge with Oneness. You are the divine. Every part of you is One.

As you move slowly back into your body, you will retain all that you have experienced in this meditation of the four treasures. Feel the power of each of the Elements as they flow through you. You are the Elements of power, and the Elements of power are you. Feel the Earth in your bones, the Air in your breath, the Fire in your eyes, and the Water of your emotions.

After a few minutes of feeling the Elements within you, come back to the present moment, moving your hands and feet, and slowly opening your eyes.

Take a few minutes to write the highlights of your experience in your notebook. If you like you can create an astral altar with magickal treasures much like the four treasures of the Tuatha De Danann. You can mentally fashion your sword, spear, cauldron, and stone, and then place them on your astral altar. By doing so, you both expand your imagination and deepen your connection with the four Elements of power.

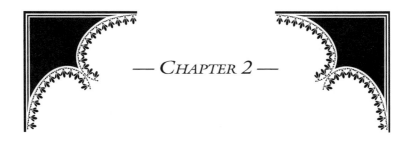

CHAPTER 2

THE GODDESS AND GOD

The Celtic Goddesses and Gods are much like the divine pantheons of other peoples such as the Norse and Greeks. The Tuatha De Danann, also called the Tribe of the Goddess Danu, were the group of people who, through their heroic deeds and adventures, became the bright Goddesses and Gods of the Gauls. The Formors, who owed their allegiance to the Goddess of the abyss called Domnu, became the dark Iberian Goddesses and Gods. Interestingly both supernatural camps had their own Druids. Together, the Gaelic Goddesses and Gods formed the Celtic archetypes. These archetypes represent the universal principles of mother, father, lover, foe, mentor, deceiver, warrior, and so forth.

Dagda's Cauldron

One of the four treasures brought to Ireland by the Tuatha De Danann was the Cauldron of Dagda. It originally came from the mythical city of Murias. The Cauldron, also called "The Undry," was an early version of the Holy Grail. Celtic scholar Charles Squire in his book, *Celtic Myth and Legend*, writes, "So great and various has been the inspiration of this legend to noble works both of art and literature that it seems almost sacrilege to trace it back, like all the rest of King Arthur's story, to paganism." But whether the scholars like it or not, to paganism it is traced!

In Celtic lore, Dagda's Cauldron is a fantastic cauldron of fertility and inspiration. Long before the Holy Grail became the cup of Christ, the Cauldron of Dagda likewise was overflowing and fed all who came to it, could heal any wound, and brought the dead back to life. Even today, the cauldron symbolizes the sacred vessel of abundance and good health in Celtic Druidism.

Most people are familiar with the stories of King Arthur and Merlin the wizard, but what they don't realize is that the stories of Camelot are actually a retelling of the original stories of Celtic mythology. As with the tale of the Holy Grail, these earlier stories were then rewritten and the names of Celtic Goddesses and Gods were changed. This process of adapting Celtic mythology into the romantic stories of King Arthur began in the Middle Ages with Geoffrey of Monmouth and Sir Thomas Malory, and continued in more modern times by Alfred Lord Tennyson and Marion Zimmer Bradley. For example, it was Tennyson, in *Idylls of the King*, who wrote that Arthur was the king who sent forth his knights to ride abroad redressing human wrongs.

One of the earliest Welsh texts, *The Mabanogi*, contains no references to King Arthur. Instead it contains the stories of the Celtic God Gwydion, whose exploits sound remarkably like those later attributed to Arthur. This similarity runs so deep that the Gwydion and Arthur myths are identical in everything but name. This recycling and retelling of the earlier stories seems to be a common occurrence with the early Celts, and has continued into modern times. The tale of Camelot is a perfect example of this because it gets reinvented with every new generation, expressed in the number of movies that recount—yet always alter—the basic story.

Besides Gwydion, other Celtic Gods and Goddesses that were rewritten in the stories of Camelot include the Celtic God Lludd, who, in Sir Thomas Malory's *Morte D'Arthur*, changes into King Loth. Also, Malory bases his Arthurian Knight Gawain on the Welsh God Gwalchmei and Sir Mordred corresponds to the Celtic God Dylan, whose father is Gwydion.

Celtic Goddesses who appear in the tales of Camelot include Numue, a Water Goddess, who Malory says is the "lady of the lake." This is the enchantress who captures Merlin's heart. Tennyson calls her Vivien, the Celtic Goddess of light, while Squire says they are both the Horse Goddess Rhiannon in disguise.

Like Arthur, Merlin—or Myrddin as he is sometimes called—is not that noteworthy in early Celtic mythology. Only later in the retelling of the original Celtic stories does Merlin appear as a main character. In these later tales, he becomes an archetypal figure. He is the ultimate Druid magician, well versed in the teachings of the art and craft. Merlin is a later version of Math, the Celtic God who could hear anything in the world and was the protector of his nephew Gwydion. This again corresponds to Merlin's relationship with Arthur.

Because there has been so much rewriting of Celtic mythology, many of the names have been changed, adapted, or omitted, depending upon the tradition. Different Druid traditions have their own favorite sets of Goddesses and Gods. These sets are sometimes different, overlap, and have different names for the same basic Goddess and God. In this way, the names of the Mother Goddesses change depending on the tradition, but at the same time many of the stories and teachings remain consistent.

The Gwyddonic Druid tradition uses Kerridwen as the Mother Goddess. She is the "white lady." ("Kerri" means "lady" and "dwen" means "white.") She is a lady of the ancient ways and the keeper of the cauldron of rebirth.

The Greatest One Kerridwen

Lately, a rebirth of feminine energy has emerged that corresponds to a renewed interest in the Goddess. The basic teachings of the Great Goddess Kerridwen are instructions describing the birth of the Goddess energy and how this energy works. From that which has no name issued the All-Mother, Kerridwen. More than creation, these instructions also explain the polarities of energy and aspects of deity. The polarities of light and dark continue, perpetuating the cycles of life. These cycles express themselves in the three-fold aspects of the Goddess: birth, life, and death (rebirth).

The instructions give the names of power for the Bright and Dark aspects of the Goddess Kerridwen, and the qualities of the Bright face and Dark face of The Greatest One. They also mention the Sky-Gods who descended to the Earth, and the fact that the Celtic Mother Goddess was originally solar, stellar, lunar, and planetary.

The Instructions of Kerridwen

1. Out of That Which Has No Name issued She who is the Mother of All Things.

2. The Greatest One, the Mother of us all did take upon Herself two Aspects: One which we call the Dark One, and that which we call the Bright One.

3. This was done so that there would be an ever re-newing of all things, and that all things might ever grow; learning from what has passed before.

4. And the Dark One took upon Herself three As-pects, and likewise did She who is Bright.

5. This was done so that in all things whether Bright or Dark, there would be a beginning, middle and end; youth, middle age, and old; negative, neutral, and positive; birth, life, and death. For all things are governed by the Great Goddess in this man-ner: dormant, greening, and harvest.

6. The Greatest One caused us to long for She who is Bright more than She who is Dark, for if it were not so, there would be no life. They who seek She who is Dark live not long, for it is Her nature to give them Death.

7. Now these are the Names of the Greatest One and Her Aspects: Kerridwen is the Name of She who is All Things; next are the two Aspects called Kerridwen the Bright, and Kerridwen the Dark. Of the Three Aspects of Kerridwen the Dark are these names: Cliodna, Morgana, and Gabba, and those of the Bright are Nimue, Bridget, and Anu. Their physical feathers are that of daughter, mother, and grandmother; and also daughter,

mother, and hag. Before the coming of the Sky-Gods, She was Sun and Moon, but now they say She is only the Moon. But to us She is still All Things. Ayea, Ayea Kerridwen!

The Story of Kerridwen and Gwion Bach

Celtic Mythology mirrors the experiences and basic teachings of the ancient Druids. Certain concepts continually arise. First is the concept of the sleepers or sleeping kings such as King Arthur. In this concept, there is a built-up power in the Earth that is waiting to be summoned in times of need. Besides Arthur, the Finnians also wait to be awakened from their chambers in the land. This concept is echoed in the original Gods of the Tuatha. When they are defeated by the Milesians, they retreat into the mounds and hills of Ireland.

The second concept revolves around the idea of the quest as portrayed in the Grail Quest. As humans, we all have a personal quest or mission that we set out on at birth. Within this quest we encounter and hopefully overcome the obstacles that we meet along the way.

The third concept involves the human aspects of the Celtic Goddesses and Gods. Like the Greek and Roman deities, the Celtic deities exhibit human virtues and faults. What makes them seem superhuman is their use of magick to achieve what they want. Often the results of this blending of human characteristics with magickal abilities creates interesting consequences.

Kerridwen and Gwion Bach's story is one of shapeshifting and the mythical chase that goes on between female and male energies. This dynamic interplay of energies is what moves the world forward on a daily, monthly, and yearly basis. Within Oneness, energetic polarities move things, much like an electric motor moves back and forth between the positive and negative poles. It is the basis behind the theory of alternating current, an idea that for the most part powers all the machines you use at home and work.

The Gwion Bach's story begins when the nobleman Tegid Foel marries Kerridwen, who is learned in the three arts of magick, enchantment, and divination. They have a son, who is particularly ugly, and because of this they initially call him Morfran, meaning "Great Crow," but later change it to Afagddu, meaning "utter darkness." As a mother, Kerridwen knows she must do something if her son is to ever achieve his noble heritage, so she turns to her magickal arts for a way to remedy the situation.

She finds a way that combines the knowledge of Earthly herbs with human effort and cunning. By gathering certain herbs at particular times, she puts together a magick potion in her cauldron that must be stirred continually for a year and a day. After this time, she is told that three drops will come forth that will give the receiver mastery of the arts, coupled with the gift of prophecy.

Kerridwen puts all the herbs into the cauldron, and then hires an old blind man to stir the pot. She also hires the lad leading the old man to add kindling and stoke the fire under the cauldron. As I mentioned earlier, the cauldron is a magickal tool, and the lad known as Gwion Bach knows this, so after a year and a day, he moves Morfran out of the spot Kerridwen had set him in, and stands in the spot himself. The three magickal drops then fall on Gwion Bach instead of Morfran.

When Kerridwen hears of it, she goes after Gwion Bach in what is called the "Magickal Chase." In order to escape her, Gwion shapeshifts into a hare. Kerridwen shapeshifts into a gray hound, and pursues him. After shifting many shapes, Gwion becomes a grain of wheat, and Kerridwen a chicken who devours him. After carrying him in her belly for nine months, Gwion is born again as Taliesin, the greatest of the Celtic Bards. Once he is born, Kerridwen becomes his protector, and the relationship changes from one of conflict between the two of them to connection.

As with the concept of the sleepers, ancestral energy is very important in Celtic Druidism. Our ancestors pass their power to us in our blood, as well as giving their power to the land, to the Earth, when they die. This power, both within and without us, waits to be awakened and used again.

The Goddess and Her Consort

The female and male energies converge at conception and the moment of creation. From this beginning, they interplay in choreographed sequences that make up life's patterns. Within Celtic Druidism, this association is expressed in the relationship of the Goddess to her consort. The relationship forms a pivotal steppingstone to understanding Celtic Druidism.

The polarities of male and female energy converge together into One, forming the basis for balance and harmony in our world and the universe. The Druid tradition explains that every female aspect has a complementing male aspect or consort.

The idea that the consort or male energy derives from the Goddess or female energy is exactly the opposite of the Christian concept of Adam and Eve, where God fashions Eve from Adam's rib. The Gwyddonic Druid concept concurs with the natural order of things. The female is the one who gives birth and is the vessel of creation. Within this context, all things, including the consort, arise from the Mother of All Things.

The Consort

This is how it was explained to me. The Great Kerridwen, Mother of All, wished to set an example for humankind, and so she created a husband for herself and she called him Kernunnos. For every aspect of the Goddess, there is also a consort. She fixed his nature to the seasons so that in the Winter his bright nature slept while his dark nature roamed the land. But after Yule his bright nature would begin to awake and would fully awaken when the Spring Equinox came around. And his bright nature would rule for the full season of the greening. When the green things came to fruit, and began to die, it was time for his dark nature to rule again, and for his bright self to enter his winter sleep.

The eight Great Days of Power remind us of Kernunnos' progress through the seasons. If you have ever been in the woods and suddenly a strong fear comes over you for no reason, it is his dark presence that has come upon you. Pray to Kerridwen the Bright to protect you by repeating "Kerridwen, Kerridwen, Kerridwen," and leave the area quickly.

Shapeshifting

As told in the story of Kerridwen and Gwion Bach, shapechanging is something that every Celtic Goddess and God can do. In a more holistic sense, all the other Goddesses are all aspects of the Mother Goddess and the Gods are aspects of the consort. The Mother Goddess and her consort shapeshift into their many personas as they move through the year; at Yule, it's Kerridwen and Kernunnos, at Lughnassad, it's Rosemerta and Lugh. Throughout the year the faces of the Goddess and God shift shape according to the seasons.

When you merge with the Celtic Goddesses and Gods, you in turn become a shapeshifter. At this point you're able to become anyone you desire, because everyone is an extension of yourself, much like each Goddess is an aspect of the Mother Goddess. You become who you want to be by connecting with things and becoming one with them. When you struggle with your world, you're struggling with yourself. When things don't work, you need to change them, and change is what shapeshifting is all about.

As a living being, you constantly change and because of this, it is important to regularly reinvent who you are. This re-invention is an integral part of shapeshifting. Every day when you get up, shower, and dress, you are shapeshifting into a new persona. During the day, you may put on many faces, depending on the situation. Shapeshifting is the ability to change into the best shape at the best time to achieve maximum results, for example, shifting into a tiger at an important sales meeting.

Many of the Celtic Goddesses and Gods are connected with various animals and the Elements. By shapeshifting and becoming One with a specific animal or Element, the Goddess or God gains more power. You, like deity, can also shapechange into helpful power animals.

Shapeshifting can empower and motivate you. Often your conditioning encumbers who you can be. You see yourself in a certain way, which has more effect on you than any other opinion or approval you can ever hope to receive. You need to like who you are, or everything else is wasted. By becoming other shapes you can do a little exploring and see yourself as you are, and the ordinary world for what it is. Seeing the world from its many angles and perspectives is what shapeshifting is all about. By becoming all things and merging with Oneness, you get in touch with your true nature.

The Sacred Head

The sacred head is like a computer, meaning it's a source of constant information that moves beyond time and space. In Norse mythology, Odin keeps Mimir's head much like Dagda, in Celtic mythology, keeps Bran's head.

The classic example of the sacred head is told in the *Mabanogi*, in the tale of Bran and Branwen, the Children of Llyr. In this story, while battling the Irish, Bran is mortally wounded in the heel just like the Greek god Achilles. He asks that his head be cut off and buried at the White Tower of London. The seven who remain in Bran's party do so, first taking Bran's head to Harlech for seven years and then to Gwales (Grassholm, Pembrokeshire) for 80 years, where Bran's head converses with them and tells them what's going to happen in the future.

When Bran instructs his comrades to cut off his head, he becomes an instrument of prophecy. Again this points to the message that prophesy derives from the human connection to the divine. The sacred head is symbolic of that connection.

The human head contains two of the chakras—the third eye and the crown chakra—which both have a spiritual nature to them. Because of this, the head connects human beings to their higher spiritual nature. To sever the head is to severe a person from his or her spirituality and connection to the Goddess and God.

The head of Bran the Blessed was buried under the White Tower to protect Britain from invaders. This is the basis for the legend that if the ravens leave the Tower of London, Britain will be invaded, as Bran's name means "raven." It is interesting to note that no foreign invader since 1066 C.E. has successfully invaded Celtic lands.

Celtic Goddesses and Gods

When doing ritual and magick, you invoke divine energies to assist you. These divine energies have particular characteristics and aspects that make them unique.

I have divided the following list into three basic parts. The first part is the main Celtic Goddesses and Gods, which gives you a jumping-off point for working with the various deities. The second part lists one Irish and two Welsh families of Goddesses and Gods, and how they relate to one another. The third part is an alphabetical listing of the Celtic Goddesses and Gods and their qualities.

Every Celtic tradition has its own Tuatha of Goddesses and Gods. Often these names overlap into the various traditions. I have tried to include many of these cross-references.

The Main Goddesses and Gods of Celtic Druidism

This first list is useful for becoming familiar with the more prominent Celtic Goddess and Gods. Every Celtic tradition has a name for the "Mother Goddess." In the Welsh tradition I was initiated into, Kerridwen is the name of the Mother Goddess. Because of this I have listed her and her consort, Kernunnos, first.

Kerridwen–

> In the Welsh Gwyddonic tradition, she is the All Mother, a Goddess of inspiration and knowledge, called "The Ninefold One." She is the crone Goddess with prophetic powers. Her magickal symbol is the divine cauldron of inspiration of the Otherworld. Her totem animal is the sow.

Kernunnos–

> In the Welsh Gwyddonic tradition, he is the All Father and a God of wealth. He is lord of the forest, animals, and a God of life and death. His magickal symbols are antlers, horns, a serpent belt, and a bag of coins. His power animals are a stag, a bull, a rat, and three cranes.

Danu (Also Dana, Anna, Anu, Don)–

> A Goddess of wisdom and control over all things, air of air. She is the ancestral deity and Mother Goddess of the Celtic people, representing complete abundance. The Tuatha De Danann are the Children of Don, and originated from the cities of Falias, Gorias, Finias, and Murias. The Children of Don were Nemedian survivors who returned to Ireland. Danu is one of the Dea Matronae of Ireland and a Goddess of fertility. Her magickal symbol is a staff.

Dagda–

> He is a chieftain and Great Father called the Mighty One of Knowledge. A lord of wisdom, Dagda is the Good God or the Good Hand, a master of life and death, and bringer of prosperity and abundance. Twin to Sucellos as ruler of the bright half of the year, he is father to Bridget. The power and knowledge from the Dagda is given as a breath called the "awen" by a kiss to

the one he chooses as successor as Chief Bard of the Druids. The "awen" is the breath of the God (the Dagda) that guides and instructs, and that sets a bard apart from others. The Dagda's gifts are the rods of command, a chalice, a magick harp, the flesh hook, a sword, club, and an inexhaustible cauldron that satisfies all hunger.

Math– Son of the mysterious Mathonwy, and a great king and powerful Welsh God of wisdom, sorcery, magick, and enchantment, he is a master Druid, teacher, and shapeshifter. Math symbolizes the cycle of birth, life, and rebirth. His feet rest in the lap of a virgin, and one of his abilities is being able to hear anything once it is carried on the wind.

Lugh (Also Lug, Lleu, (Llew) Llaw Gyffes)–
Called "Lugh of the Long Hand," he is the uncontested master of all arts, and a God of war, justice, smiths, poets, and bards, associated with the setting sun and the mysteries of the moon. Lugh is a fertility God and champion of the Tuatha, historian, and powerful sorcerer. His symbols are the cock, turtle, goat, a bag of coins, magick spear, and sword. His spear gave victory in battle, and his sword was called "The Answerer." Lugh's foster mother is Tailtiu, and he is the grandson of Diancecht and Baler of the Evil Eye. He is the son of Ethniu and Dagda, consort to An the Triple Goddess, and the father of Cu Chulain.

Families of Goddesses and Gods

All families stem from the Mother Goddess. From the Mother come the family branches of the Goddesses and

Gods. Like most families, they represent the polarities of human character. The important thing to remember is that each Goddess and God represents an aspect that you can recognize within yourself and within others.

Sometimes when doing ritual, it helps to work with a particular family of Goddesses and Gods. Other times, you may want to draw one divine aspect from each family. The reason this is important is because ancestral ties rest at the foundation of Celtic Druidism.

One of the main Gaelic or Irish families descends from the Dagda, whose name means the "Good God." The Dagda's immediate family includes his wife Boann, and children Bridget, Angus, Mider, Ogma, and Bodb the Red.

Boann (Also Boi, Boanna)–

Mother of Angus, she is a river Goddess who gives her name to the River Boyne. Wife of Elcmar, the Dagda desired her and sent Elcmar on an errand that was made to seem like one day but actually lasted nine months. She is associated with the silver salmon and white cows. She is also "mother of the herds."

Bridget (Also Brigit)–

She is a sun and fire Goddess, fire of fire. Associated with the lambing season and the coming of Spring, she is the Goddess of the hearth and home and represents the sacred fire. She is a Goddess of smithcraft, healing, medicine, poetry and inspiration. Her symbols are the spindle and distaff, the sacred flame, a fire pot, and her brass shoe. She was the first to use the whistle for calling another at night.

Angus (Also Angus Og, Oengus)–

His name means "Young God." He is a God of love and intimacy, and Boann's son, fostered by Midir. Because of his magickal conception, gestation, and birth, he has power over time. He is an eternally youthful symbol of love and beauty. His kisses become birds that hover invisibly over young men and maidens, whispering words of love into their ears.

Mider (Also Midir, Midir the Proud)–

A Gaelic God of the Otherworld or Underworld called The Faery King, Mider is the son of the Dagda and Boann, and brother to Angus, Bodb the Red, Lugh, Ogma, and Bridget. A bard and chess player, he likes to play games for high stakes. He is a Celtic Pluto and consort to Etain. Associated with the Isle of Man and the Faery hill of Bri Leith, he has three wonderful cows, a magick cauldron, and owns the "Three Cranes of Denial and Churlishness." The three cranes stood beside Mider's door, and when someone came by to ask for hospitality, the first one said, "Do not come! Do not come!" Then the second crane said, "Get away! Get away!" The third one added, "Go past the house! Go past the house!"

Ogma (Also Ogmios, Cermait ["honey-mouthed"])– Called the Binder and Trenfher, meaning champion or strong man, he is the God of literature, eloquence, and the inventor of the Ogham staves. He is said to be of sun-like countenance, lusty, well-endowed, handsome, and very knowledgeable. His symbols are a club, stick, and the oghams.

Bodb the Red–

> A son of the Dagda and Boann, he is virile and athletic and represents active male energy. He succeeds his father as King of the Gods in later legends, is King of the Sidhe, and Bard of the Tuatha de Danann.

The Children of Don

Known as "the Children of Don," another name for Danu, this Welsh family of Goddesses and Gods stem from Don (Danu), who is the Mother of the Tuatha De Danann. Her brother is Math, and her son is Gwydion. Don's daughter is Arianrhod, who has two children Dylan and Llew. Two of Don's other sons are Gobannon and Nudd.

Gwydion– The son of Don (Danu), he is a God of kindness, the arts, eloquence and magick, a master of illusion and fantasy, and helper of humankind. He is the brother of Gobannon, Arianrhod, and Amaethon. Math, son of Mathonwy, passes on his infinite knowledge and abilities to his student and nephew Gwydion. Bard of the Tuatha De Danann, he is a wizard, healer, prince of the powers of the air, master harpist, and shapeshifter.

Arianrhod–

> A star and moon Goddess similar to Sirona, she is the daughter of Don (Danu), and sister to Gwydion, Gobannon, and Amaethon. A Goddess of higher love and wisdom, she represents elements of Air and Water. "Arian" means silver and "rhod" means wheel or disc. Her symbols are the crescent moon, stars, and moonbeams. She is the keeper of the "Silver Wheel" or "Silver Disc,"

which is a silver wheel with eight spokes that represents the wheel of the stars. Her palace is the Corona Borealis, which is called Caer Arianrhod (The Northern Crown).

Dylan– A water God who can swim as well as a fish, he is also called "the Son of the Wave" because no wave ever breaks beneath him. God of magick, fertility, and magickal children, his uncle, Gobannan, accidentally kills him.

Lleu (Also Lleu Llaw Gyffes)–
A Sun God and shapeshifter, he is the Welsh counterpart to the Irish Lugh. His name means light. His deceptively beautiful wife Blodeuwedd was created for him by Gwydion and Math. His palace near Bala Lake is called Mur y Castell. His totem animal is an eagle.

Gobannon (Also Govannon, Gobannan, Goibniu, Goibhnie, Goibnll)–
He is a blacksmith God of magick called "Gobban the Wright" and Gobban Saer, "The Master Mason." The divine smith works with metals and forges, and his symbols are blacksmithing tools and the transforming fire.

Nudd (Also Lludd, Nuada, Lludd Llaw Ereint)–
A Celtic Zeus and aspect of the All Father who was often called "The Good Father," Nudd is consort to Fea, the powerful war Goddess. He is a chieftain God of wealth, war, rebirth, kingship, and thunder, and has a silver arm made by Diancecht. Nudd was the first king of Tara, and his symbols are a magick spear, thunder, and lightning. He carries the sword from Findias, one of the Tuatha De Danann's four treasures.

The Children of Llyr

The other main Welsh family of Goddesses and Gods descends from Llyr, whose name means "the sea." One of his wives is Pendardun, a daughter of Don. With her, he fathers a son Manawyddan, who is identical with the Irish Manannan Mac Lir. His other wife is Iweridd (Ireland), who has a daughter named Branwen and a son named Bran.

Llyr (Also Ler, Lir, Lear, Leer)–

A God of the sea and ocean king, Llyr is also a God of music. He is husband to Aebh and Aoife, and father to Manawyddan, Finonuala, Creiddylad, Hugh, Fiachra, Morgana, and Conn. He is a shy God who rarely reveals himself and can appear as part man and part fish. He is very gentle and loving, but if provoked can rage. His symbols are seashells, and his power animals are sharks, sea mammals, the sea serpent, and sea gulls. He plays a harp of silver, pearl, coral, and shell.

Manawyddan (Also Manannan, Manannan Ap Llyr, Manannan Mac Llyr, Manannan Mac Lir)–

He is a God of the sea, travel, and magick, a master shapeshifter and great teacher. He is consort to Fand, Rhiannon, and Aife. The Land of Promise, an Elysian island, is his home. His symbols are a wand, a magick coracle, a magick spear called Red Javelin, and several magick swords, three of which are named The Great Fury, The Little Fury, and Retaliator.

Iweridd (Also Iweidd)–

An Irish Goddess and wife of the sea God Llyr. Mother of Branwen and Bran the Blessed. Her name means Ireland. She and her husband Llyr are connecting links between the Gaelic and Welsh.

Bran (Also Bran the Blessed, Bron)–

He is so big no house or ship is big enough to hold him. He is one of the giants with magickal treasures that enrich Britain. Besides being a fierce warrior, he is also a protector of poets and bards. Associated with the sacred head, the inexhaustible cauldron, and prophecy, Bran is a bard, harpist, and singer. His power animals are the crow and raven.

Branwen–

A Welsh Goddess of love called the White-Bosomed One and the Venus of the Northern Sea, she is the daughter of Llyr. Branwen's name means White Raven and was the title of the love Goddess in Wales and Cornwall. She died of a broken heart and was buried by the river Alaw, in Anglesey. Her power animal is a white crow.

Other Goddesses and Gods

This is a listing of Celtic Goddesses and Gods that you can use when doing magick and ritual. Depending on your intention, choose the Goddess or God who can most help you. Keep in mind that they are all aspects of the Mother Goddess.

Aebh (Also Aobh)–

A Goddess of Ireland who was the wife of the sea God Llyr, her son is the shapeshifter, Aed Mac Lir.

Aife (Also Aifa, Aoife)–

Called the Princess of the Land of Shadows, she is a Celtic Queen associated with Scotland and a rival of the Amazonian queen Scathach. She is defeated by Cu Chulain and his son. Also the consort of the sea God Manannan and mother to Connla, she is associated with the swan, crane, and the alphabet of knowledge.

Aine–

A primary Earth and solar sovereignty Goddess of Ireland associated with the Summer Solstice, she is still worshipped on Midsummer's Eve and appears on St. John's Night. Queen of the Faeries and woman of the Side, she is a Goddess of love, fertility, and desire. She is the daughter of Danann Owel, wife and sometimes daughter of Manannan Mac Lir, and mother of Earl Gerald. As a powerful sorceress, her magickal symbols are the "red mare," fertile crops, cattle, and the wild goose.

Amaethon–

He is a wild husband-man and God of agriculture and the harvest. The Welsh word for farmer is "amaethwr." Called the Harvest King, his symbols are the fruits of the harvest and farmer's tools, particularly the sickle, hoe, and plow.

Andraste (Also Andrasta)–

She is an Icenian warrior Goddess of victory, war, fertility, life, and death. The British have sanctuaries dedicated to the Goddess Andraste in a sacred woods, like the forests of the Island of Mona (Anglesey). She is associated with the hare.

Arawn–

He is the Welsh king of Annwn (Annwfn), the Brythonic Underworld; The Land Over Sea, Land

Under Wave, Caer Sidi the Revolving Castle. He is a shapeshifter, God of death, rebirth, ancestry, and war. He sent the swine to Pryderi, and is associated with the cauldron, sweet water springs, magickal beasts, the ancestral tree, and the pig.

Artio– She is a bear Goddess and the monad of all female bears. The bear controls temporal power. A fierce protectress of nature, King Arthur's name "Artos Viros," meaning bear man, comes from this Goddess. The constellation of the Plough or the Great Bear is called Arthur's Wain.

Badb (Also Badhbh, Badb Catha)–

A Gaelic Goddess of war, wisdom, death, and inspiration, she is the wife and sometimes granddaughter of Net, a war God. As an aspect of the Morrigan, she is the Battle Raven, and her name means Scald-crow. She fills warriors with fury and helped defeat the Formorians in Ireland. Her father is Ernmas and her sisters are Macha, the Morrigu, and Anu. Her symbols are the cauldron, ravens, and crows.

Balor– He is a sun God and king of the Formors, who were the early giants, originally occupying Ireland. Son of Net and grandfather to Lugh, he has a baleful eye that, when opened, lays waste to his enemies. At the second Battle of Mag Tuired, Lugh puts out Balor's evil eye with a sling-stone and kills him.

Banba– An Irish Earth Goddess representing the sacred land, she is part of the triad of the three Goddesses of sovereignty that also includes Folta and Eriu. She is wife of MacCruill, and thought to be the first settler in Ireland. One of Ireland's ancient names is "the island of Banba of the women."

Belinus (Also Bel, Belanos, Belenus)–

A God of life, truth, war, inspiration, and music. His mother is Corwenna and his brother Brennius. He represents fire of fire, and is said to have been buried in a golden urn in London. An active healing (dry heat) God, he drives away diseases. His symbols are the roadways, sun disc, a golden harp, and a golden curved sword and spear.

Belisama– The Goddess of Fire and an aspect of Bridget, she is known as the "young sun" and the "sun maiden." Her name means like unto flame or bright and shining one. Her symbol is the rising sun.

Belisana– An aspect of Belisama with a similar appearance, but more earthy, she is a solar Goddess of healing, laughter, and the forests.

Blodenwedd (Also Blodewedd, Blodeuedd)–

A sun and moon Goddess associated with the dawn and the May Queen, she is called "Flowerface" or "White Flower." Created by Math and Gwydion from flowers, blossom, and nine elements, she is the most beautiful and the most treacherous Goddess, and is associated with the Arthurian Guenevere. She is turned into a white owl by Gwydion. Her magickal symbols are the white owl, meadowsweet, oak, broom, primrose, and cockle.

Borvo (Also Bormo, Bormanus)–

>A Celtic Apollo and a God of healing, he is asso-
ciated with wet heat, such as hot springs and mineral waters. He represents the elements of Fire
and Water, and is a God of unseen or concealed
truth and inspiration through dreams. His symbols are a flute, a golden harp, a golden sword or
spear, hot springs, and the sun disc.

Brigantia–

>A powerful Celtic Briton nature Goddess of
Water and pastoral activities with distinct similarities to the Irish sun Goddess Bridget, her name
is an ancient name for the rivers and the curves
of the countryside. She is a titular Goddess of
the Brigantes in Yorkshire.

Camulos (Also Camulus)–

>A Celtic Mars and war God associated with clouds
and storms, he carries a large sword. Coins with
his name on them carry the symbol of the boar.

Cliodna (Also Cleena)–

>A seagull Goddess and young aspect of the dark
Goddess. Her name means shapely one, for she
is the most beautiful woman ever seen when she
takes human form. Her symbols are an apple and
three magickal birds. A great wave from the sea
swept her away to the Otherworld of the Faeries
at a place on the southern coast of Ireland. Because of this, she rules the ninth wave of every
series of waves.

Cordemanon–

>A young, handsome God of travel, knowledge,
and dreams, he is associated with stone circles,
books, the quill, alphabet, and archives.

Coventina–
A river Goddess of childbirth, renewal, and healing springs, she is a triple Goddess. Her well in Carrawburgh, Northumberland, represents the womb of the Earth. Her symbols are the well, cauldron, and cup.

Credne– A God of craftspeople, metal workers, smiths, and wrights, he is associated with Gobannon (the Divine Smith) and Luchta (the Divine Wheelwright). A Master Swordmaker known as "The Bronze Worker," he helps forge the Tuatha de Danann's weapons and helps Diancecht make Nuada's silver hand and arm. His symbol is a bronze sword.

Diancecht–
Grandfather to Lugh and physician of the Gods, he makes Nuada's silver hand, but kills his son Miach. His tools are the mortar and pestle.

Dumiatis (Also Dumeatis)–
A master teacher God of creative thought and like a Celtic Mercury, he tells teaching tales and is associated with children. His symbols are the quill pen and ink, writing staves, and books.

Edain (Also Etain)–
A Goddess of sovereignty, grace, and beauty, she is the wife of Mider, won by him in a chess game. Heroine of ancient myth, she is an example of transmigration, reborn with the same identity as her original self. Be-Finn means "Beautiful Woman" or "White Woman" and is the surname of Etain. Faeries in certain folk traditions are called the "White Ladies." She is associated with the Otherworld, a herd of white mares with blue eyes, and apple blossoms.

Elayne (Also Elen, Elen Lwyddawg)–
She is the Leader of the Hosts and considered the Warrior Mother, also called Eriu, Goddess of Ireland. A Goddess of war and leadership and of immense stature. Myrddin is one of her consorts.

Epona– An Earth fertility and horse Goddess representing fertilization by water, she is a protectress of horses and their riders. She is a Goddess of birth, life, death, and rebirth, often associated with fruits such as the apple, with corn, and serpents.

Eriu– A Goddess of sovereignty of the land like Banba and Fodla, she is an ancient Earth Goddess representing Ireland and a Queen of the Tuatha De Danann. As a solar Goddess, she hands the golden cup filled with red wine to the successive kings of Ireland. This signifies their union and the fertility of the country. A beautiful woman and shapeshifter, she can shape warriors from clods of earth. The poetic name for Ireland, Erin, means "the land of Erui."

Esus– A woodland God and aspect of the dark face of Kernunnos, he is a woodsman and hunter who slays Tarvos, the golden bull. He carries an ax, bow, and sword.

Fagus– He is a tree God representing the monad of all beeches.

Fand– Called the Pearl of Beauty, she is a great Faery Queen of Ireland and wife of the sea God Manannan. She is a shapeshifter, daughter of the sea, and ruler of the "Land Over Wave." Her magickal symbol is the seagull.

Findabair–

A Goddess of Connacht and the Otherworld, who represents beauty and love, she is the daughter of Queen Medb and her consort King Aillil. Findabair the Fair married a mortal man named Fraech against her father's wishes. She died of a broken heart when her lover was killed by Cu Chulain.

Fliodhas– A Goddess and protectress of the woodlands and woodland animals, associated with the deer Goddess Sadv, she calls the wild animals of the woodlands her cattle. Her symbols are a large doe, green grass, trees, and woodland springs.

Gabba (Also Gabis of the Abyss)–

She is a crone aspect of the Dark All Mother and one of the dark queens. She is the Goddess of the 13th moon. Her name means "Crystal." No one knows or remembers what she looks like because to look at her face kills you. Her symbol is the Celtic endless weave and quartz crystals.

Gwalchmei (Also Gwalchmai)–

He is the nephew of King Arthur, son of the Goddess Mei, and is called the Hawk or Falcon of May. He portrays a God of love and music. His symbols are hawks and the fields at hunting times.

Gwyn ap Nudd–

A God of the Wild Hunt, he is a God of the death chase and the Otherworld. He is the hunter of souls and lord of the unmanifested. He has a white hound with red ears named Dormarth.

Hellith– A God of the setting sun (Fire and Air), and of the dying. When invoked, he brings peace to those near death. After death, souls are in his protection until they reach their destination. His symbols are the setting sun disc and a flute that brings peace and tranquility to those who hear it.

Hertha (Also Herdda)–
She is an Earth Goddess, representing the greening of Spring. A Goddess of rebirth and healing, her symbols are the cow and calf and a milk pail.

Letha– A harvest Goddess associated with Midsummer, her magickal symbols are a swan and apples.

Luchta (Also Lucta, Luchtaine)–
A God of smiths, wrights, and craftsmen who is associated with Gobannon, he is the Carpenter God and shieldmaker for the Tuatha.

Mabon (Also Mapon, Maponus)–
A Celtic sun God of prophecy, he is associated with light and the wild chase or ritual hunt. As the son of Modron, he is the great son (sun) of the Great Mother. He is taken from her when he is three days old. Called "The Son of Light" or "The Divine Son," he represents youthfulness, sex, love, and magick, and enjoys playing tricks. Associated with Myrddin and later Christ, his symbols are the boar, mineral springs, and the lyre.

Macha– A powerful Irish threefold sun Goddess of war, fertility, and ritual games, she was wife of Nemed and consort of Nuada; called the "Sun Woman." Ancestress of the Red Branch, Macha is a Queen of Ireland, daughter of Ernmas, and granddaughter of Net. Her body is that of an athlete, and her symbols are the horse, raven, and crow.

Medb (Also Maeve, Mab)–

A Goddess of sovereignty, she is the good queen called The Warrior Queen. She is the Faery Queen and Queen of Connaught. She runs faster than a horse, while carrying animals and birds on her arms and shoulders. She also carries a spear and shield.

Mei (Also Mai, Meia)–

An Earth and sun Goddess, similar to Rosemerta, she is the mother of Gwalchmei.

Modrona (Also Modron, Madrona, Matrona)–

A Goddess associated with Coventina, Morgana, Vivian, and Dechtire, she is an aspect of the All Mother. The Great Goddess and Mother of Mabon or "Light."

Morgana–

A Goddess of war, fertility, and magick, she is the Death Mother and Queen of Death. Born of the sea, she is the daughter of Llyr and Anuand, a powerful shapeshifter. She is beautiful and sensuous. Her symbols are trees along shoreline, especially cypress trees, seashells, ravens, and crows.

Morrigan (Also Morrigana)–

She is called the Great Queen, Sea Queen, and the Great Sea Mother. As a powerful Goddess of wisdom and the sea, she is associated with the queen's rod of command, sand dollars, ocean vegetation, manta rays, and whales.

Morrigu– A Goddess of death, life, music, and magick, she is called the Dark Gray Lady. She protects sailors and the shores of Erin and plays a harp made of silver, shell, and pearl.

Myrddin– A sun and Earth God, Fire of Earth, he is a God of the woodlands, nature, and mirth. A Sky-God associated with stones, caves, crystals, and magick, as well as herbs, natural mineral deposits, and pure water springs, his symbols are the wild rose and sweet water springs. He plays a flute whose sound makes you want to dance.

Nantosuelta–
A Goddess of abundance associated with Sucellos; she is a river Goddess. She holds a dove house on a pole in one hand, and carries a baker's paddle.

Nemetona–
A warrior Goddess of the oak grove, she is the great protectress of the sacred nematon. Also a patron of thermal springs, her symbols are oak groves, a ram, and a spear made of ash with a tip of silver.

Nimue (Also Niniane, Niviene, Nymenche)–
An Earth and Water Goddess and a young aspect of the Bright All Mother, she is a Goddess of lakes also known as the Lady of the Lake, maker and keeper of Excalibur, King Arthur's sword. She is consort, student, and teacher to Myrddin. She created the river, Ninian, that originates in the Cotes-d'Armor in Brittany. Her symbols are a white-silver sword, underwater caves, swans, swallows, and quartz and crystalline formations.

Nodens– A God of sleep, dreams, and dream magick, he is a God of the Otherworld.

Nwyvre– A God of the ether, stars, and space, he is also God of celestial sciences, astronomy, and astrology. Consort to Arianrhod, his symbol is the nine-pointed star.

Pryderi– A master of disguise and shapeshifter, he brought the swine from the Otherworld. He is the son of Rhiannon, and associated with the pig or boar.

Rhiannon–

A Goddess of knowledge and an aspect of the All Mother. She is called Queen Mother and is associated with horses as the Queen Mare. She was originally called Rigatona or the Great Queen. Her symbols are apples, a mare, and three birds.

Robur– A God of forests, in particular oaks, he is the monad of all oaks. He is a tree God known as the Forest King, and is depicted with mistletoe tangled in his hair and beard. His symbols are a budding oak staff and woodland animals.

Rosemerta–

A Goddess of abundance and plenty, she is Lugh's wife and a young aspect of the All Mother. Her symbols are fertile gardens, flowers, and a cornucopia filled with good things.

Sadv– A Goddess of the forests, she is called "The Deer Goddess." Mother to Oisin the poet, her totem animal is a doe.

Sirona– A Celtic Venus of astral nature, she is a stellar and solar Goddess. Her consort is Borvo. She is usually depicted with a small dog. Healing Goddesses were often associated with dogs because the lick of a dog was thought to have curative powers.

Smertullos–
A God of the abyss and associated with the unmanifested, he is called The Preserver and Lord of Protection. His symbols are a snake with a ram's head and a snake belt.

Sucellos– A God of life, death, and fertility, he is the Dagda's twin and ruler of the dark half of the year. He has such beauty that to look upon his face would bring death, so he appears in many disguises and shapes. His carries a large spear.

Taillte– An Irish Earth Goddess of August and Lughnassad, she is daughter of the King of Spain, foster mother to Lugh, and lives on the magickal Hill of Tara. Teltown is named after her as are the Tailltean Games (Irish Olympics).

Taliesin– A Welsh Bard, prophet, the greatest poet, and master shapeshifter, he is the son of Kerridwen. He foretells many of the future events in British history, and is thought to be the scribe of the Gods. He is a writer of poetry and music, and a magick maker. The quill, riddles, and harp are his symbols.

Taranis– A God of the passing seasons, storms, and thunder, he is associated with the eight-spoked wheel of the year.

Tarvos Trigaranos–
A God of vegetation and a young aspect of Kernunnos, he was born at Coventina's well. His symbols are willow or oak and three gray cranes.

Tethra–   A shadowy God of the sea and magick, representing the elements of Air and Water. He is associated with the albatross and seagulls.

Ti Ana (Also Ty Ana, De Ana, Dy Ana)–
A Goddess of the house and home, her name means "Thy Mother" or "Ana of the Household."

Triana–   As the Threefold Mother, she represents the three faces of the Goddess. Sun-Ana is a Goddess of healing, knowledge, and mental arts. Earth-Ana is a Goddess of nature, life, and death. Moon-Ana is a Goddess of higher love and wisdom.

Viviana (Also Vivian, Vivien)–
A Goddess of birth and life, she is a bright Goddess of life and love, of mothers, childbirth, and children. Her name means Life Mother, and her symbol is the five-petaled red rose.

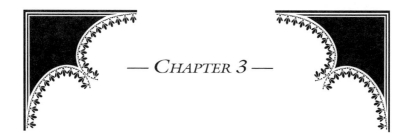

THE PRELIMINARIES

You will need to complete a few specific tasks before your initiation into the Celtic Druid tradition. First, gather your ritual tools together, and second, choose a teacher who can either be someone that has successfully done the Five Magickal Works (see Chapter 6) and is willing to teach you, or a divine teacher willing to guide you through the works. Many people chose to have both a mortal and divine teacher. The third task is to find your craft and totem names, and the fourth is to do the Secret Name Work. Upon completing these preliminary tasks, you are ready for your initiation.

Gathering Your Tools of the Art and Craft

Filled with the divine light of the Goddess and God, your ritual tools are essentially alive and a part of you. You consecrate them, place them on your altar, and use them regularly until your ritual tools become a part of you. Using your tools triggers whole-brain activity, which helps to induce a state of consciousness conducive for magick making. They help to create a doorway to the Otherworld.

By tradition, before your initiation, you gather together six tools, plus your robe and cord. The tools are the wand, athame, chalice, bowl, incense burner, and candle holder. Avoid selecting any tools made from plastic. Metal, stone, wood, glass, and other natural materials all conduct energy better than plastic.

During initiation, place your altar tools under, or to the left (Goddess side) of the altar (see the Altar Table Diagram on page 106). In the Gwyddonic Druid tradition, the High Priestess and High Priest approve and consecrate the initiate's tools immediately after initiation. As the seeker, you bring your tools to the High Priestess and Priest who are going to perform your initiation, and say:

> Here are my tools of the Art and Craft.
> I love the Goddess and I desire her path.
> I pray that you accept me and find me not lacking.

The High Priestess and Priest charge your ritual tools with sacred energy by merging with Oneness, with the Goddess and God. They direct sacred light into the tools. When working solitary, you can merge with Oneness and with the divine light of the Goddess and God yourself, and charge your tools with sacred energy.

Be sure to clear all unwanted energies in your tools prior to your initiation, for example, by smudging them, passing them carefully through the flame of a sacred fire, or rinsing them in salt water.

The Robe

Whatever color and style, notice how much time you take selecting or making your robe. What does your robe say about who and what you are? Your craft robe is like the first house of the zodiac, representing your outward form. It is your skin, fur, scales, and feathers. It is not the custom to go sky clad in the Gwyddonic Druid tradition.

Each of the Goddesses and Gods appear in different colored robes. For example, Sun-Ana wears a white robe with a bright yellow mantle, clasped at her breast with a golden sun disc; Earth-Ana wears a green robe with a brown mantle, fastened with a copper broach in the shape of three green leaves; and Moon-Ana dons a gray robe with a blue mantle, clasped with a silver crescent moon.

You can either make or purchase a ritual robe, with or without a hood. The robe represents the Water element and is usually a solid color, sometimes trimmed in a contrasting color. Select a robe in your favorite color, or in a color that harmonizes with your favorite Goddess or God. Women often wear full-length robes. Men often prefer short-belted robes or tunics that can be worn over their slacks.

My mother made my first craft robe, which was a deep rose color with dark purple sleeves. The colors I selected were in honor of the Celtic Goddesses Rosemerta and Morgana. I was also given a second craft robe made of natural cotton, which I now use for Spring rituals in honor of Bridget.

After your initiation, it is customary to sew, embroider, or paint a green pentacle on your sleeve or cuff. The symbols are put on a woman's left sleeve and a man's right sleeve. They designate degree of knowledge as follows:

First Degree

Second Degree

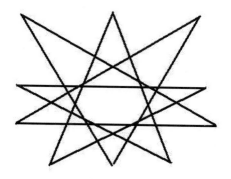

Third Degree

Craftmaster

The Cord

In ancient times, priest astronomers used the rolled measuring cord and rod to assure the precise astronomical orientation of temples. In the Druid tradition today, the cord can be used like a compass to mark the boundaries of your sacred circle. In addition, you can also wrap it around the waist of your craft robe.

Representing the Earth element and symbolizing the cord of life, the cord can be of any material and color. I chose a deep purple cord because I have always felt drawn to this color.

The Gwyddon cord is nine feet long with a total of five knots. First, knot both ends. One end knot can be a loop so it can be attached to a stick. Then tie the middle knots at four-and-a-half feet, six-and-a-half feet, and seven-and-a-half feet from the end with the loop knot.

The Wand

Associated with the East and the Air element, the most ancient of ritual tools is the wand. An extension of your mind and hand, it is used in magick to bridge dimensions and direct energies in specific ways.

Merge with the Air element when you make your wand. This will strengthen its magickal power. Follow these 12 easy steps to make your own Druid wand.

1. Select a branch from a fruit-bearing tree such as apple or oak for your wand.

2. Find a living tree to cut your wand from. (If the tree is on someone else's property, ask permission before cutting the branch.) Cut only as much of the branch as you need for the wand.

3. Communicate with the tree. Sit under it, and notice everything about it, its scent, shade, bark, trunk, branches, leaves, and even its voice as the wind moves through it.

4. Walk around the tree clockwise three times. As you do this, ask it if you can have a branch from its body. You should get some sense of yes or no. If you sense a negative response, find another tree, and ask again.

5. Before cutting your wand, dig a small hole in the ground at the tree's base. Pour an offering such as honey and milk into the hole, and thank the tree spirit.

6. Cut your wand after the moon has gone dark, at dawn or at twilight on a day of the new moon, and up to three days following. Timing the cutting in this way will give the right amount of "curing" time. The wand length is usually measured from the outside bend of your elbow to tip of your finger. Snap the wand off the tree or cut it with your athame, and be sure to take the appropriate precautions so you don't cut yourself.

7. Use your athame to shape your wand and strip off the bark. Keep the bark shavings on a cloth or piece of newspaper.

8. During the next 28 days, go back and put the bark shavings around the base of the tree. Do this in a clockwise circle, and thank the tree again. Sing a blessing song or chant to the tree as you walk around it.

9. Leave the stripped wand outside or in a window in the moonlight for a moon cycle, new to full, shaping it a little each day.

10. Once the wand has dried, seal it with consecrated oil. Use oil with the qualities you want in your wand. (For example, a wand sealed with rose oil would give the wand loving energies.)

11. You can leave your wand as it is or decorate it. For example, you can mount crystals in the wand tip. Choose stones with the qualities you want in your wand. You can also cover the wand's body with strips of fabric like silk or cotton, wind ribbon over the shaft, or attach feathers, shells, and small bells to it.

12. Carve or paint your wand with runes, oghams, or Theban symbols. (Please refer to the appendices.) Use the names of the Goddess and God such as Kerridwen and Kernunnos, the wand's name, or your craft name. Use your athame to carve names. You can also use consecrated oil or the ashes of burned runes to trace the symbols on the wand's body.

For my craft wand, I selected a branch from a tree I passed by every day on the way to work, but it proved to be too brittle to work with. I then chose the branch from a birch tree outside my backyard. It took me four evenings to strip off the bark using my athame, but the process was well worth it. I used newspaper to hold the shavings, and then returned them to the tree while quietly singing a song of thanks.

I oiled my wand with honeysuckle oil nine times, each time writing its magickal name along the wood with the oil. I then let it dry. I put a clear quartz point at the tip, and several tiny gemstones such as aquamarine, tourmaline, golden topaz, and amethyst along the shaft. Next, I glued two flicker bird feathers toward the base, and then tied them down with a red silk cord.

The Athame

A double-edged ceremonial blade made of silver, steel, iron, bronze, copper, brass, or stone, the athame can be worn on your power side, hung on the cord of your robe. Usually purchased new, it is the tool of the South direction, representing the Fire element. The athame is used to lay or cut the Great Circle when beginning ritual. No self-respecting Druid would ever use her or his athame to kill or eat with. It's a sacred tool!

Some athames are small, some large, some more sword-like, while others are more akin to daggers. I have seen everything from letter openers to antique blades, to handcrafted ceremonial knives and swords used in circle. For myself, I selected a small boot knife as my athame.

Many people dull the blades of their athames, but wait to dull your blade at least until after you have cut and stripped the bark from your wand. I never did dull the blade of my craft athame, but the ceremonial blade I use on the altar is dulled, making it much safer to use in ritual. Remember to keep all blades in a safe place, away from young children and away from the edges of your altar table.

It is the Gwyddonic Druid custom to carve, write, or paint the names of Kerridwen or Kernunnos on the handle of your athame in runes, oghams, or Theban. You can also name your athame, for example, "Firestar," and engrave that name on its blade. You can put your craft name on it as well. (Please refer to the appendices.)

The Chalice

The chalice is the sacred vessel that holds the Water element. Some Druids feel that the Water element represents all directions, not just the West, because it flows in all directions. In the Gwyddonic Druid tradition, Water is most often associated with the West.

The chalice holds water, wine, or juice during rituals and magickal works. Traditionally made of clay or metal, once consecrated, the chalice becomes a loving cup, embodying the sacred union of the Goddess and God. It represents the magickal cauldron, the grail, the source of life, and the well of inspiration. From its watery depths, all things emerge. I initially choose an antique pewter chalice for my own use, and then found out it was made from pewter with lead in it. I then switched to a crystal wine chalice and now use a hand-made stoneware chalice.

The Bowl or Salt Dish

Symbolizing the womb of the Mother Goddess and traditionally made of clay, the bowl corresponds to the North direction and the Earth element. It can be a watertight bowl, dish, large shell, or cauldron. The universal purifier—salt—usually dry, and sometimes mixed with water, goes into the bowl. You can also use soil in your bowl.

My first craft bowl was a simple white soup bowl that my Nana had given me. I now use a six-inch brass bowl etched with the image of a flying dragon that was a gift from my mother-in-law.

The Incense Burner

Burning incense symbolizes the element of Air, activated by Fire. Your burner needs to be large enough to easily burn a sheet of paper in. Make sure your burner has a sturdy handle or chain that can be grasped because it is moved during ritual.

A pot pad is advisable when the burner is hot and smoking. Because of the renewed popularity of incense, the number of burners to choose from has increased, including ones decorated with dragons, Goddesses, faeries, wizards, suns, and stars.

New Age shops, health food stores, and gift stores all sell convenient incense cones and sticks you can use, or you can buy the small charcoal rounds, choose some favorite herbs, and burn them over the charcoal. To avoid burning your fingers, I suggest you use a pair of tweezers to hold the charcoal round when lighting it. You can use a layer of sand or pebbles inside the burner as a base for the charcoal round(s). I like to grow my own herbs and flowers, dry them, and then sprinkle them onto the burning charcoal one at a time.

If you are allergic to smoke, you can use an aromatherapy diffuser instead of incense. Diffusers and oils can be purchased at gift and department stores, New Age shops, and health food stores.

The Candleholder or Candlestick

The lighted candle represents the Fire element, transformation, and the creative source. You will need a candlestick and a white candle for your initiation and magickal works. Placed in the middle of the altar, the lit white candle represents the Goddess.

Altar candleholders are usually made of metal or clay, but you can also use glass and crystal ones. Taper, votive, pillar, and specially shaped candles are all readily available at most grocery, discount, New Age, and department stores. As with any magickal tool, use your intuition when choosing your altar candles and candlesticks.

My first candleholders were made of blue glass, one a sky blue, and the other two, cobalt blue. I collect candlesticks, and over the years have found many unusual ones that I use in rituals, for example, a brass holder shaped like a pine cone.

Additional Craft Tools

+ **Altar cloth**. Traditionally red, its color can also match the changing seasons. Used to cover and protect the Lady's Table (the altar surface) from dripping wax.

+ **Pair of candlesticks**. During rituals, a green candle representing the Goddess is put on the left/feminine side of your altar, and a red one representing the God on the right/masculine side. This means you will need two additional candlesticks with candles for doing rituals. Please refer to the Altar Table Diagram on page 106 for placement.

+ **Wine chalice**. Use to drink wine from at rituals. Engrave or paint a personal symbol or your name in runes on your wine chalice.

+ **Goddess and God images**. Objects and images that represent the Goddess and God such as statues, plants, stones, pictures, and so forth.

+ **Sword**. Rarely worn, the sword is a tool of ancestry. It is used like the athame.

+ **Staff**. Used as a wand, the ritual staff can be carved or painted with runes, ogham, or Theban. Often it is named for particular Goddesses and Gods, such as Myrddin's Staff.

+ **Book of Shadows**. A journal, notebook, or binder in which to write notes, works, and ritual experiences.

+ **Food, music, scented oils, and decorations**. These can all add more power to your magick.

Unconventional Tools

The traditional tools are tactile and sensory. I also suggest creating some unconventional tools such as tools on your computer screen. These have a different "feel" to them because they are technological rather than tactile. I have created Goddess and God symbols, plus a graphic wand and chalice with my computer paint-and-draw program. Be creative and have fun!

Consecrating Your Magickal Tools

Magickal tools are focals, given energy and life by the power of your thoughts as you merge with them and the Divine energy of the Goddess and God. You can consecrate your tools by merging deeply, with the intention of placing divine elemental energy into them. Do this by becoming One with the Goddess and God, and asking them to impart their Divine energy into the specific tool. Imagine the power of the Goddess and God moving into the object. Use rhythmic breathing to deepen your merge. Your breath and intention help to direct the divine energy into the tool.

Washing your altar tools with dew before sunrise on Beltane morning fills them with divine creative power. As well as using dew to consecrate your tools, you can also use the four great Elements of Earth, Air, Fire, and Water to charge your ritual tools and other items with powerful elemental energies. You can set them out in the sun and moonlight, for example, or rub them with herbs and oils to enhance their power.

Athames, swords, staffs, and wands, can be consecrated at sunrise, noon, dusk, or midnight, on one of the eight Great Days. Take each tool separately and work with it for a few minutes. Literally breathe energy into the tool three times. Imagine and sense your energy and the elemental energy flowing into the tool and empowering it. Use a candle, fire, or the sun as a focal for putting divine Fire energy into your athame. For example, work facing south in a well-lit area, preferably outside at sunrise or noon. One of the best times is at sunrise on Hertha's Day or Beltane. Use the power of the sun's birth to fill yourself and then your athame with Fire energy.

Sprinkling cool vervain tea on your magickal tools while chanting a blessing song is another way to consecrate them. Called the enchanting herb, vervain empowers all magick making. It protects against negativity.

You can also consecrate your tools by rubbing them with fresh rosemary, basil, oak leaves, or lavender flowers at sunrise, noon, or dusk. After rubbing the tool, lay it on the ground and point it toward the direction it represents. For example, point your athame toward the South. Walk around the tool sun-wise (clockwise) three times. As you do this, scatter fresh bay leaves over the tool. Pick up the tool and hold it upward in the direction it is associated with. Ask that the tool be filled with the divine power of the Goddess and God.

✦ **To consecrate the bowl,** fill it with earth, and hold it upward toward the North point of your sacred space, and say three times:

> Generous and divine powers of Earth,
> Charge this tool with your sacred energy.
> I ask this in the name of the Goddess and God.
> Blessed be! So be it!

✦ **To consecrate your incense censer,** hold the censer upward toward the East point of your sacred space, and say three times:

Generous and divine powers of Air,
Charge this tool with your sacred energy.
I ask this in the name of the Goddess and God.
Blessed be! So be it!

✦ **To consecrate your candleholder,** hold it upward toward the South point of your sacred space, and repeat three times:

Generous and divine powers of Fire,
Charge this tool with your sacred energy.
I ask this in the name of the Goddess and God.
Blessed be! So be it!

✦ **To consecrate your chalice or cup,** hold each one upward toward the West point of your sacred circle, and say three times:

Generous and divine powers of Water,
Charge this tool with your sacred energy.
I ask this in the name of the Goddess and God.
Blessed be! So be it!

✦ **To empower your tools even more,** pass them through, or sprinkle them with the corresponding Element. For example, pass your candleholder through the flame of a candle, or sprinkle water on your chalice. When doing this, say:

With this Element,
I consecrate this tool to the Goddess and God.
Blessed be! So be it!

Smudging Your Sacred Space

It's a good idea to purify your ritual space, altar, and tools by smudging them before and after ceremonies. An herbal mixture of sage and cedar, sometimes blended with lavender, copal, or sweetgrass, the smoke of these herbs cleanses your altar, tools, and yourself of unwanted energies.

Loose sage or smudge sticks are available at most health food and New Age stores. You can also grow or gather sage and cedar, drying the herbs, and either tying them in sticks or using the loose dry herbs. For a smokeless alternative to smudge, use sage and cedar oil in an aromatherapy diffuser. You can also put a few drops of both sage and cedar oil in a pan or bowl of boiling water to smudge your space without smoke.

To use a smudge stick, begin by lighting it and then blowing on it softly until it starts to smoke. Hold the burning smudge over a fireproof bowl or dish as a certain amount of the burning herbs drop down as thick, hot ash. Pass each of your tools through the smoke, and say:

> May all evil and foulness be gone from this tool.
> I ask this in the Lady's Name.
> May the Great Goddess,
> Protect and bless this sacred tool,
> And fill it with her divine light.
> Blessed be! So be it!

When you finish smudging, douse the stick in water to put it completely out. Do not allow it to smolder!

Choosing a Divine Teacher and Sponsor

Before being initiated into the art and craft, it is customary to select a Goddess or God to be your divine teacher, companion, and advisor. Refer to the list of Goddesses and Gods in Chapter 2, and make your selection based on your needs and desires. For instance, if you choose Modrona the Great Mother Goddess as your guide, she may teach you about the sacred forces of the land and sea, as well as the universal patterns and cycles of the cosmos. Granddaughter of the god Belenus, the all-knowing Modrona is the Mother of Mabon, the son of Light. Her father, Avallach, is the King of Avalon, where she lives with her sisters and cares for the land. Associated with the sovereignty of the land, and similar to Coventina and the Morrigan, Modrona is a sorceress and healer, and protects sacred springs, fountains, craftspeople, and artists. Her magickal symbols are children, flowers, and fruit, and she embodies the lifeforce and fertility, as well as maternity and the creative energies of nature.

I selected Gwydion as my divine teacher. He is God of the creative arts and master shapeshifter. He presented himself to me as a young shapeshifting God in an initiation dream I had early one morning just weeks before being initiated. I asked him his name in the dream, and he told me he was called Gwydion and that he had much to teach me. After telling me his name he took off a mask he was wearing and as I looked into his eyes, I found myself looking into my own eyes.

Dreams are excellent ways to find a divine teacher and sponsor. One way to access the dream world and its knowledge is to give yourself the suggestion to dream of your divine teacher and sponsor. Repeat the suggestion to yourself aloud at least nine times just before going to sleep and again immediately upon waking: "I will discover who my divine teacher and sponsor are." Do this for a period of 28 days, or a complete moon cycle, to assure meeting your divine helpers in your dreams.

Your sponsor acts as your protector and ally and looks out for your best interests while filling you with divine power, especially when you make a genuine effort to gain rapport.

For my divine sponsor, I choose the Goddess Triana because I felt she represented my higher self. She is the Threefold Mother, and wears three faces of the Goddess: 1) Sun-Ana, who is a Goddess of healing, knowledge, and mental arts; 2) Earth-Ana, who is a Goddess of nature, life, and death; and 3) Moon-Ana, the Goddess of higher love and wisdom. Whenever I need to gather knowledge or skill, I commune with Triana. She is a strong balancing influence in my life.

Choosing a Craft Name

Part of the metamorphosis of becoming a new individual is choosing a craft name. Your craft name is a magickal name. It represents the spiritual you—the you who has been re-born through initiation. It is the name used for rituals and things associated with crafting magick. For many initiates, selecting a craft name is a way to let go of all your past con-ditioning attached to your given name. For others, craft names are like double identities. Choosing your craft name is an act of magick. You are solely responsible for selecting your name. While it might be a good idea to ask the opin-ions of other people when choosing a name, don't ask some-one else to name you.

Some people select a simple craft name, others select mul-tiple and complex names. You might find your name in a book, from the skies, in nature, or you can use the name of your favorite Goddess or God. Your imagination is your only limit. Pick a name you like! Many of these names have been used for thousands of years, and there is specific energy and per-sonality associated with them. Select a name that empowers you and allows your magickal self to flourish, a name you can gracefully grow into. It should conjure up positive images of the attributes of the name itself. For example, if you choose the craft name Bridget, it would encourage you to take on the beneficial qualities of the solar Goddess as well as strengthen those "Bridget" qualities that you already possess. For this reason, be sure to know both the positive and negative qualities of the craft name you select and be honest with yourself as to the reasons you are taking the name.

My first craft name was "L'Achren" from a mythological reference to the poem attributed to Taliesin called "The Battle of Trees," referred to in Robert Graves' book, *The White Goddess*. Gwydion has to guess Achren's name in order to pass the threshold. I took her name and coupled it together with the "L" rune. As you continue in your studies of the art and craft, you will discover your first name no longer represents you. At this time, it's perfectly alright to select another name to use in ritual. Since taking my first name, I have chosen a total of four other names. Here are some ways to find your craft name:

1. Ask, "What is my craft name?" just before going to sleep at night. Tell yourself that you will remember the name upon waking.

2. Look through books or surf the Internet for Goddess and God names. Select a special one that you feel drawn to.

3. Sit in front of a candle and gaze into the flame, or use a mirror to gaze into the flame. Do this for several minutes, all the while asking what your craft name is. Use deep, rhythmic breathing to relax you even more. Often a name will come almost immediately.

4. Sit under a tree for a few minutes, and ask the tree for the wisdom to know your craft name.

5. Take a ritual bath, with scented oils, candles, and inspiring music. While you are bathing, ask the Goddess to reveal your craft name to you.

Choosing a Totem Name

Your totem name is in addition to your craft name. Swan is one of my totem names. I chose this name after a dream experience I had that included the constellation Cygnus. The swan is related to the family of Llyr, one of the branches of the Mabinogi. The shapeshifting of humans into swans is a recurring element in Celtic mythology.

Legend says the ancient Druid Craftmasters used the magick power of "faet fiada" to become invisible to those who they didn't want to see them. "Faet fiada," literally meaning "the appearance of a wild animal" and frequently called shapeshifting, was one of the shamanic talents of the Tuatha De Danann and the Druids. Often this shapeshifting phenomena was connected with totem animals and the powers and wisdom therein.

The word totem translates as "from kin, my kin, her kin, his kin." As sacred animals, totems are regarded as mythical ancestors, protectors, and friends. Because of this, I find it personally distasteful to eat my friends, and hence, I became a vegetarian. As you learn to mirror the faces of the Mother, you gain knowledge about the patterns of nature. By cultivating rapport with the energy of a totem, the wisdom of the sacred animal passes into you. Remember that rapport with several animal totems is possible. For example, the master shapeshifter God Manannan's animal forms include the dolphin, falcon, panther, and wolf, among others. Following are the steps for choosing a totem animal name:

1. Select a particular bird or animal with which you feel a strong kinship. For instance, I chose the swan as one of my totem animals and names.

2. Study the animal as much as possible. For example, I read books, looked at numerous photos, movies, watched swans move in the wild, and read folklore pertaining to the swan.

3. Compose and perform a "Totem Naming Ritual" in an effort to deepen your relationship with the totem.

4. Express your true desire for kinship with the totem. State aloud all the efforts you are willing to make and the knowledge or skill you desire in return.

5. State aloud that you are the totem animal, the totem is you, that you are one. In my case, I stated, "I am the Swan, the Swan is me, we are one."

6. Ask your totem animal to guide you in your dreaming and waking states, to be your helper and messenger.

7. Repeat steps 1 to 6 a minimum of three times with each totem animal you select, or that selects you.

The Secret Name Work

As you may have guessed, names are sacred and can be used as magickal aids. Once initiated, you perform the Secret Name Work as a means for protection against any negativity or magickal attack. You merge with Oneness and discover a special name for yourself, a name that has always been your name. Your secret name arises out of the "Eternal Now," from a point where you can see anything and find everything. Over and over again, speak aloud to yourself, preferably someplace where no one else can hear you. Address your essence and ask your inner self to reveal your secret name to you, a name representing your true being. Many names will come to mind, but make an effort to hone in on the one name that keeps coming up. You may find your secret name in your dreams. You should have no doubt as to your true name. Use your intuition in this process, and be sure to NEVER tell anyone your secret name, and NEVER write it down. There are NO exceptions.

Once you know your secret name, you are ready to become this new name. Compose and perform a private "Ritual of Naming" to strengthen your secret name's magickal protective power. Be sure no one can hear or see you when doing this ritual. Use the following steps.

1. State aloud that you are now known by your secret name [say the name], and that all the previous names you have been known by are not really your true names. Only one name represents the true you, and that is your secret name [say the name].

2. State aloud in your ritual that no one can harm you with any negative work of magick unless they know your true name. [Say your secret name again.]

3. Create an eternity clause in your Secret Name Ritual and work by setting up impossible tasks that would have to be performed by someone who discovered your secret name and wanted to use it against you. For example, say aloud, "Before anyone can use my secret name against me, they have to count all the atoms, one by one, of all of the celestial bodies of the cosmos over and over again, backwards and forwards, forever and a day."

4. Repeat steps 1 to 3 a minimum of three times. Each time you perform your Secret Name Work, you reinforce a pattern or shield of strength, protecting yourself from negativity. Remember, NEVER write down your secret name or tell anyone what it is.

After you complete your "Ritual of Naming," you may feel like a different person. This is natural side effect of the ritual. When performed correctly, you become, in essence, a new person with a new name. Your secret name becomes a powerful ally and shield as you progress in your Druidic studies.

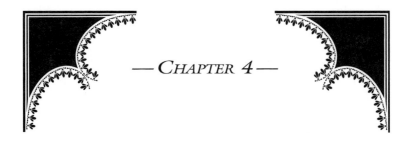

CHAPTER 4

INITIATION

Initiation means "to begin." In the Gwyddonic Druid tradition, it is when you begin learning the basics of the art and craft. I remember being extremely nervous before my initiation. This is normal, so remember to enjoy the experience as much as you can. After all, it's not a scary experience. Your initiation is a celebration. You are being reborn!

Taking the Sacred Oath

Before you are initiated, you take a special oath. In ancient times, groups of individuals took oaths. These oaths tied them together into one tribe or clan. In the Gwyddonic Druid tradition, it is customary to take just such an oath called "the Sacred Oath." You say aloud,

> "I promise to worship no other Gods
> But the Gods of the Tuatha Kerridwen."

This is the oath I took during my initiation. When I took it, I was promising to work in rapport with Oneness. For this reason, I am also comfortable working with deities from other spiritual traditions such as Egyptian, Greek, Norse, Roman, Sumerian, Hebrew, Native American, and Christian. It is all One.

Keep in mind that the Sacred Oath is binding, but optional. By no means is it necessary to take an Oath to use the teachings. It's your choice. If you feel a kinship with the Tuatha, you may choose to take the Oath as a way to reaffirm your connection with the Celtic Goddesses and Gods.

You can also create a personal Sacred Oath, something that expresses your spiritual intention and connection with Oneness. For example, "I promise to move toward Oneness," or "I promise to carry the light forward." Whether traditional or original, be aware that you are responsible for the oath you take. You are making a sacred promise.

Setting Up Your Altar

The altar is a sacred space, a place where you can communicate with the divine. A working surface for ritual and magickal works, the altar is called the Lady's Table. It holds your magickal tools and other items. Just gazing at the altar with its lit candles, ritual tools, and burning incense creates a magickal state of mind.

One of the best kind of altars is one made of stone. Representing the Earth and the North direction, stone grounds all unwanted energies. Metal or wood altar surfaces are also good choices. I use a wood table, the counter top, or the entertainment center. Any sturdy and stable table, mantle, bookcase, or desk can also be used for your altar. Whether or not you leave your altar set up after working magick is entirely up to you. If you have young children, I suggest you put your athame, sword, herbs, and incense, as well as oils, lighters, matches, and anything else that can harm them, safely away after rituals.

In the Gwyddonic Druid tradition, it is customary to set your altar up in the North sector of your sacred circle. The alternative sector is the East, which corresponds to the rising sun. Some people prefer to set the altar up in the center of the circle. I suggest that you try different placements, and then choose the one that works best for you.

Altar cloths are most often red or green, but they can be any color. As far as fabric, your cloth can be made of cotton, silk, velvet, or wool. You can also embroider or paint the runes, ogham, or Theban on your cloth.

Arranged for practical and magickal purposes, the Gwyddonic Druid altar uses certain objects to represent the Elements. In the West is Water, which forms a semicircle with the Elements of Earth, Air, and Fire. The left, Goddess side of the altar holds the nurturing Elements. These are the chalice of Water and the bowl of Earth. Green, lavender, or silver candles, and something that represents the Goddess, are placed on the left side. The God side holds the power Elements of Air and Fire. Red, gold, or orange candles, an image or symbol of the God, and the other masculine ritual tools such as your athame, incense burner, and sword are all placed on the right-hand side. The wine chalice rests at the center point. It is a symbol of divine love. From the Goddess, the wand (Air) points in the direction of transformation (Fire). The athame stems from the God side and points toward the cooling Water element. The wand also points in the direction of manifest energy (things that are), while the athame points in the direction of unmanifest energy (things yet to become), representing the cycle of life. Please refer to the Altar Table diagram on page 106.

Altar Table Diagram

NORTH

GODDESS IMAGE		GOD IMAGE
GREEN CANDLE		RED CANDLE
	WINE	
SALT (BOWL)	WATER (CHALICE)	INCENSE (BURNER)
	WHITE CANDLE	
WAND		ATHAME

W E S T

E A S T

SOUTH

Design your altar to correspond with the seasons, changing items such as stones, flowers, candle colors, and so forth. Place all of your tools and other items you will need for the ritual or magickal work on the altar where you can easily reach them. While you are setting up your altar, think about what you are doing and what the tools represent. Next, be sure to light the candles and incense before you begin your ritual or work. The candles should be allowed to burn down safely on their own, or you can snuff them out when you are finished, and then burn them all the way down the next day.

Modern Druids don't put things like skulls, bones, or furs on their altars because the altar is the sacred table of the Goddess. No dead thing is placed on it.

Opening the Great Circle

The Great Circle is a divine bridge. In the Gwyddonic Druid tradition, the Great Circle is a closed circle, not open as in some traditions. The chance of negative energies penetrating a closed circle is very remote. Because of this, I sometimes leave the circle down during the night, and then pull it up in the morning. I find this enhances my dream experiences. Whatever your preference, just be sure that you eventually pull up the circle when you finish. Follow these six steps for drawing the Great Circle before doing the initiation ritual, Great Day rituals, full moon rituals, and before doing magickal works:

1. Prepare your sacred working space by putting salt in a bowl of water, and then take a sprig of greenery and dip it into the salt water.

2. Sprinkle your altar and ritual area in a clockwise circle starting at the North point, and moving in a circle to East, South, West, and back to the North. As you do, this say out loud in a clear voice,

> May all evil and foulness
> Begone from this place.
> Begone from this place
> In our Lady's name!
> Begone now and forevermore!

While saying this, imagine a cobalt blue and white light energetically clearing the area out.

3. Face the altar and knock on it nine times with the base end of your wand, in three sequences of three.

4. Mark the Great Circle by using your cord. Start at the center point of your circle. Move outward with your cord, marking each of the four corners of North, East, South, and West. You can use clear

crystal points or other stones to mark your circle. Use the same stones every ritual, and don't clean or clear them out. They will act as energy collectors of your sacred ritual experiences.

5. Standing at the center point of the circle, use your athame to draw or cut the Great Circle. Do this by pointing your athame outward and then merging with the blade, the Fire element. Your intention is that the athame tip is a laser beam of bluish-purple light. Start at the North point, and draw a circle of bluish-purple light while slowly spinning in a complete clockwise circle.

6. With your anthame, cut an energetic door (one made with intent and mind energy) in your circle just below the East point. This is called the "Little Gate." You, and anyone else present during rituals, enter and exit through this energetic door. By doing so, the energy of the Great Circle remains solid and unbroken. The stronger your circle, the more positive energy you can generate during magick making.

Calling in the Four Wards

Calling in the wards brings the protective power of the four directions and Elements into the Great Circle. The more elemental power you bring into the ritual circle, the greater your magickal success.

The key to calling in the four wards is merging. As you invite the divine energies of the four directions into your circle, merge with each Element. Follow these simple steps:

1. Stand at the North point of the circle and face outward. Take the bowl of salt (or earth) and

sprinkle three pinches of it at the North point. Place the bowl back on the altar, and pick up your athame.

2. Face North with your athame in your dominant or power hand pointed outward. Hold your arms high above your head. Merge deeply with the Earth element. Say in a firm voice:

> Oh Great and Mighty One
> Ruler of the North March
> Come, I pray you
> Protect the Gate of the North Ward
> Come! I summon you!

3. Set your athame back down on the altar, and pick up the incense censer. Wave the incense back and forth three times toward the East point of the circle. Then set it back down on the altar.

4. Pick up your athame in your power hand. Face East and merge with the Air element. Hold your arms high above your head, and say:

> Oh Great and Mighty One
> Ruler of the East March
> Come, I pray you
> Protect the Gate of the East Ward
> Come! I summon you!

5. Set your athame back down on the altar, and pick up the candle. Wave it three times, back and forth, across the South point of the circle. Then set it carefully back down.

6. Pick up your athame, face South, and merge with the Fire element. Hold your arms high above your head, and say:

> Oh Great and Mighty One
> Ruler of the South March
> Come, I pray you
> Protect the Gate of the South Ward
> Come! I summon you!

7. Set your athame back down on the altar, and pick up the chalice of water. Dip your fingers into the water and sprinkle a few drops toward the West point of the circle. Do this three times, and then set the chalice back down on the altar.

8. Pick up your athame, face West, and merge with the Water element. Stretch your arms upward, and say:

> Oh Great and Mighty One
> Ruler of the West March
> Come, I pray you
> Protect the Gate of the West Ward
> Come! I summon you!

The four wards are now set in place at the four points of the Great Circle. They are powerful, elemental beings that serve as guardians while you are making magick and doing rituals.

Preliminary Ritual

This ritual is performed before the Great Day and full moon rituals. Traditionally, the High Priest or man representing the God does this ritual, but the High Priestess or woman representing the Goddess can also perform it. Follow these five easy steps:

1. Face the altar, pick up the bowl of earth or salt, and sprinkle the altar with three pinches of earth

or salt. Hold the bowl upward toward the North, and say:

> Ayea! Ayea! Kerridwen!
> Ayea! Ayea! Kernunnos!
> Ayea! Ayea! Ayea!

2. Turn to the East, and wave the lit incense three times back and forth. Hold the incense upward, and say:

> Ayea! Ayea! Kerridwen!
> Ayea! Ayea! Kernunnos!
> Ayea! Ayea! Ayea!

3. Face South, and wave the lit candle back and forth carefully three times. Hold it upward, and repeat:

> Ayea! Ayea! Kerridwen!
> Ayea! Ayea! Kernunnos!
> Ayea! Ayea! Ayea!

4. Face West. Sprinkle the water from the chalice. Hold the chalice upward, and repeat:

> Ayea! Ayea! Kerridwen!
> Ayea! Ayea! Kernunnos!
> Ayea! Ayea! Ayea!

5. Face the altar once again, and say:

> Blessed be!
> Blessed be the Goddesses and Gods!
> Blessed be all who are gathered here!

The Wine Ritual

The wine ritual is performed before the main ritual. Using a blessed cup of wine (or juice), the ritual is clearly sexual in the way the athame enters the vessel. This helps to bring the fertile union of male (God) and female (Goddess) powers into the circle. The wine ritual lends itself to couple and group ritual. Follow these guidelines:

1. The woman representing the Goddess holds the cup of wine between her hands in front of her.

2. The man representing the God takes his athame and holds the blade above the wine.

3. Merging with the divine, he plunges the blade slowly into the wine, holding it there, and says:

> Great and Mighty One
> Let thy blessing and power
> Enter into this wine!
> So, mote it be!

4. The woman hands the cup of wine to the man.

5. Holding it upward toward the North point, he merges with the Earth element, and says:

> Ayea! Ayea! Kerridwen!
> Ayea! Ayea! Kernunnos!
> Ayea! Ayea! Ayea!

6. He turns to the East point, merges with the Air element, holds the wine cup upward, and repeats:

> Ayea! Ayea! Kerridwen!
> Ayea! Ayea! Kernunnos!
> Ayea! Ayea! Ayea!

7. He turns to the South, merges with the Fire element, holds the cup upward, and says:

> Ayea! Ayea! Kerridwen!
> Ayea! Ayea! Kernunnos!
> Ayea! Ayea! Ayea!

8. He turns to the West, holds the wine cup upward, merges with the Water element, and repeats:

   Ayea! Ayea! Kerridwen!
   Ayea! Ayea! Kernunnos!
   Ayea! Ayea! Ayea!

9. Turning toward the altar, he holds the cup upward, and says:

   Blessed be!
   Blessed be the Goddesses and Gods!
   Blessed be all who are gathered here!

10. Then he hands the wine cup to the woman representing the Goddess.

11. She drinks from it and then hands the cup to another man in the group.

12. He drinks, and then hands the cup to a woman in the group, and so forth, until it returns to the High Priest or man representing the God.

13. He drinks the remainder, sets the empty cup upon the altar, and everyone says in unison:

    Blessed Be!

Initiation

In the Gwyddonic Druid tradition, it is when you begin learning the basics of the art and craft. After showing your intention by gathering your magickal tools and taking the Sacred Oath, the initiation ceremony begins.

The initiation ceremony symbolizes the death of your old self and the rebirth of your new self. Upon initiation, you are born from a kind of sleeping death and awakened to your true self. The actual date of your initiation is significant and has an influence in your life. It's your second birthday. You also now have a second astrological chart, so make a note of the exact day, time, and location of your initiation.

Either with a group or solitary, the Gwyddonic Druid initiation consists of a formal ceremony where you are energetically reborn. This is done by crawling through the legs of a woman. Choose a Great Day on which to be initiated, and then choose your Hound.

The Hound is a person who is already initiated into a mystery tradition. The Hound leads and protects you during the initiation ceremony. He or she is the one who guides you from point to point and from Element to Element. The Hound knows the way and willingly leads you down the path of rebirth and Oneness. Your hands are bound and your eyes are covered, so you must rely on your Hound. You must trust the Hound to lead you on the right path.

The Warden in the initiation ceremony is usually the High Priestess or High Priest. She or he is the keeper of the keys to the elemental energies. Customarily, the High Priestess acts as Warden when initiating the boys and men. The High Priest acts as Warden when initiating the girls and women. It is also just as valid to have women initiating women and men initiating men. It's just a different polarity, so be aware of the change in energy. The ones who initiate you are also the ones who consecrate your magickal tools. These are put on or under the altar during your initiation so they can absorb the magickal energy of the ritual.

You can also perform a solitary initiation ceremony by choosing a divine Goddess and God to guide you through the process. I suggest tape recording the initiation ritual, reading the parts aloud, slowly and clearly. When you read the part of the Hound, leave plenty of time for you to repeat after the Hound when you play back the tape and do it "live."

Once initiated, you become a First Degree Student of the art and craft. You celebrate your new birthday and new name. My own initiation ceremony was on the autumnal equinox, on Hellith's Day and on a full moon, the Wine Moon. I recall being very nervous about the whole process, and then feeling so energized afterwards that I spent the whole night reading books on magick and mythology, until finally drifting to sleep.

Initiation Preparation

When the initiate, also called the seeker, reaches the door of a Druid College or group, she or he is customarily met with the Greeting Cup. The Greeting Cup is a large consecrated chalice filled with wine or juice. The person with the Greeting Cup says brightly, "Merry Meet and Merry Part!" and then offers the chalice to the newcomer. The initiate takes a sip, hands the wine back, and says the password, "Perfect Love and Perfect Peace! Blessed be!" Then the initiate enters.

Prior to the actual ceremony, the initiate is taken into a separate, darkened room of the house. When working outside, the initiate is taken to a private spot away from the main activity. The initiate is blindfolded, and her or his hands are firmly but comfortably bound together with a white cord or string. The initiate is then given the Death Cup to drink. Usually the Death Cup mixture is some sort of sweet liqueur blended with cranberry juice and bitters. Liquor is not necessary. The important thing is to make the drink very bitter, but not so sickening as to make the person ill.

While the initiate drinks the Death Cup, she or he is advised to think about her or his life previous to that moment: all experiences in the past, the good and bad. The initiate is advised to shed her or his old life and old forms of thinking and doing, and is encouraged to embrace the possibilities and beauty of rebirth.

The Ritual of Initiation

The Hound of Annwn guides the Soul to the North Point.

The Warden: Who goes there? Who is it that comes to this Earthen Gate? I, the Warden of the Gates, demand to know.

The Hound of Annwn:
                It is I, the Hound of Annwn, who is the Guide of Souls that stands before thy gate.

Warden: Who is that who is with thee?

The Hound: It is a lost and wandering Soul that I have guided here.

Warden: Oh Soul, what doth thou seek here?

The Soul: I, a wandering and lost Soul, doth seek entrance to the Castle of Glass that there I mayest learn the secrets of control over all material and physical things.

Warden: What is the password? Thou mayest not enter unless thou know it.

Soul: I know it, but I cannot remember it! Pray let me enter anyway.

Warden: Nay! I cannot! Depart from here and seek elsewhere.

The Hound of Annwn conducts the Soul to the West Point.

Warden:	Who goes there? Who is it that comes to this Watery Gate? I, the Warden of the Gates, demand to know.
The Hound:	It is I, the Hound of Death, who is the guide of Souls that stands before thy gate.
Warden:	Who is that who is with thee?
The Hound:	It is a lost and wandering Soul that I have guided here.
Warden:	Oh Soul, what doth thou seek here?
The Soul:	I, a wandering and lost Soul, doth seek entrance to the Castle of the Lady of the Lake that there I mayest learn the secret of control over all emotions, feelings, and desires.
Warden:	What is the password? Thou mayest not enter unless thou know it.
Soul:	I know it, but I cannot remember it. Pray let me enter anyway.
Warden:	Nay! I cannot! Depart from here and seek elsewhere.

The Hound of Annwn conducts the Soul to the South Point.

Warden:	Who goes there? Who is it that comes to this Fiery Gate? I, the Warden of the Gates, demand to know.
Hound:	It is I, the Hound of Pwyll, who is the guide of Souls, that stands before thy gate.

Warden:	Who is that who is with thee?
The Hound:	It is a lost and wandering Soul, that I have guided here.
Warden:	Oh Soul, what doth thou seek here?
Soul:	I, a wandering and lost Soul, doth seek entrance to the Castle of Fire that there I mayest learn the secrets of control over all forms of energy and power.
Warden:	What is the password? Thou mayest not enter unless thou know it.
Soul:	I know it, but I cannot remember it. Pray let me enter anyway.
Warden:	Nay! I cannot! Depart from here and seek elsewhere.

The Hound of Annwn conducts the Soul to the East Point.

Warden:	Who goes there? Who is it who comes to this Windy Gate? I, the Warden of the Gates, demand to know.
The Hound:	It is I, the Hound of Nodens, who is the guide of Souls that stands before thy gate.
Warden:	Who is that who is with thee?
The Hound:	It is a lost and wandering Soul that I have guided here.
Warden:	Oh Soul, what doth thou seek here?
The Soul:	I, a wandering and lost Soul, doth seek entrance to the Castle of Winds that I may

learn the Great Wisdom that gives control over all things whatsoever they may be.

Warden: What is the password? Thou mayest not enter unless thou know it.

The Soul: I know it! It is "Perfect Love and Perfect Peace!" Now let me enter!

Warden: Thou doest know it, but because thou doest not know its meaning thou mayest not enter in at *this* gate. But do not despair, thou mayest enter in at the "Little Gate" for those who seek to learn the Ancient Wisdom.

The Soul is moved a few steps southwise by the Hound and told to crawl through the "Little Gate." This is traditionally through the legs of a woman.

Warden: Welcome! Thou hast come a long way! Come, kneel before me and I will tell thee the true meaning of the password, "Perfect Love and Perfect Peace." First, it means the perfect love of the Goddess and the perfect peace of the God. Second, it means the perfect love of knowledge and the perfect peace of wisdom. Third, it means the perfect love of all nature, and perfect peace by being in harmony with all things, whether animate or inanimate.

The blindfold is now removed.

High Priestess: Now I [insert your name], High Priestess (or High Priest) of this college, ask thee to reaffirm thy Oath of Initiation. Repeat after me, "I swear I will worship no gods, but the Gods of the Tuatha Kerridwen." (An optional Oath: "I swear to move toward Oneness.")

The cord is cut. The High Priestess traces the outline of a pentagram with consecrated oil on the initiate's forehead, over the third eye.

High Priestess: What Druid name hast thou taken?

Soul: [You say your craft name.]

High Priestess: I, [insert name], High Priestess of this college, declare before the Ancient Goddesses and Gods that [insert initiate's craft name] is a true Druid. So mote it be!

The High Priestess puts the initiation necklace or bracelet on the initiate.

High Priestess: Rise [insert the initiate's craft name] and receive the Blessing and Consecration of the Gods.

The High Priestess crosses the wand and athame and asks the Soul to take hold of the tools with both hands and to take in as much Power and Blessing as the initiate can hold without passing or trancing out. The First Degree Student is then hugged and welcomed into the craft by those present.

(Note: When taking in the Power and Blessing of the Goddess and God, make an extra effort to use your breath and intention to absorb and become one with the Divine energy surrounding you during ritual. Be aware of the polarities of energy. When grasping the crossed athame and wand, move as much positive energy and bright light into your being as you can.)

Perfect Love and Perfect Peace

During the initiation, the Warden asks you, "What is the Password?" You, the lost and wandering Soul being guided by the Hound of the Otherworld, know it and speak it: "Perfect Love and Perfect Peace." First, it means the perfect love of the Goddess and the perfect peace of the God. Second, it means the perfect love of knowledge and the perfect peace of wisdom. Third, it means the perfect Love of all nature and perfect peace by being in harmony with all things, whether animate or inanimate.

It is in this password that you discover renewed appreciation for love and for all of the gifts in your life. With the deeper understanding of this password, you regain your natural sense of compassion, balance, and inner peace. "Perfect love and perfect peace" is the ultimate wish you can wish anyone.

Remember These Things

"Remember These Things" provides the basic guidelines for being a Druid. These guidelines were presented to me by my teacher and are customarily read aloud in a group or by yourself. When they are read at initiations and other group celebrations, they set the tone for Druid magick and cover concepts such as seeking to harm none, being gentle and kind, and punishing error without malice, as well as tempering love with wisdom and seeking no more than you need. Probably the most important of these guidelines is that all things can be done by remembering who you really are, and by looking into the divine mirror. The password of greeting that has been kept secret for hundreds of years is also provided in this text. It is, "Perfect love and perfect peace, blessed be!"

"Remember These Things" warns against rapport with the Dark One and reminds you to bring no dead thing to the Bright One, and to never give any seed or living creature to the fire. The Gwyddonic Druid tradition doesn't practice or condone sacrifice of any kind.

Remember These Things

1. A Druid knows the nature and ways of her times.

2. A Druid knows what she knows and makes no other claims.

3. She seeks to harm none, but if faced with the necessary choice between two ills, she will seek the lesser.

4. An evil doer must not be coddled, for if you do so, he will think you weak, and will seek to do even greater harm having never been shown the just consequences of his former error. Therefore, punish error, but without malice, and quickly.

5. Give not your living to thieves, but give to those that work their honest due.

6. Be gentle and kind to the helpless, whether animal or human.

7. The Dark One seeks sacrifice of the living, and loves much blood. If you serve Her, She will ever demand more and more until She calls for you in some foul way. Her favors are not easily won. Be warned!

8. The Bright One demands nothing, but is greatly pleased with gifts of good deeds done in Her name. So bring Her no dead thing, but things of beauty and love.

9. Place Wisdom first in your life rather than Love, for Love without Wisdom is often hurtful; but temper Wisdom with Love.

10. A Druid seeks to know two things, and these are what she is and what deity is. But here is a clue for the seeker: If she comes to know the answer to either of these, she will also know the other.

11. Turn no one away who comes to you seeking the Ancient Knowledge, even if you know he be evil. For if we teach only the good ones, how shall the ones in error ever change their ways? But if they misuse the Ancient Wisdom, it will draw the Dark One to them and they will bring Death upon themselves if they change not.

12. All things can be done by remembering who you really are.

13. A Druid who once knows the way, and goes astray, is like one who is up to her knees in mud. For once you have known Her, all else is blight.

14. Seek not more than you need, and you shall ever have enough, and even abound.

15. When you gather together on the nights of the Full Moon and on the Great Days, you shall greet each other with a kiss of good love and shall give this password to each other, "Perfect Love and Perfect Peace. Blessed be!"

16. No seed of any fruit that the Great Mother has brought forth, nor any living creature, shall be given to the fire, for this is the evil that those who call themselves Christians did unto us. May the Great Ones protect us!

Toasting the Goddesses and Gods

After initiations and other rituals on the Great Days and full moons, Druids toast the Goddesses and Gods. You fill their glasses with your favorite beverage. You can use water, wine, juice, tea, coffee, soda, beer, milk, and so forth in your toasting glass. Then, select your favorite Goddesses and Gods for toasting. For instance, you might raise your glass and say, "To Anu, Ayea Great Mother," or "Ayea Dagda, the Good God!" Even when practicing solitary, be sure to toast a few of your favorite deities.

I use toasting to connect my energy with that of the various Goddesses and Gods. By connecting to these divine energies, I bring them into my life and honor them as my family and friends, paying reverence to them and to Oneness. My son likes to honor divine beings from other spiritual paths such as Buddha. I find this refreshing and completely in tune with the spirit of the tradition, because Celtic Druidism is inclusive rather than exclusive. It encourages innovation and creativity.

Feasting

Along with toasting, feasts are customary where everyone joins together for a special meal. Feasting was one of the gifts the Dagda, the Good God, gave to humankind. The feast is a sacred meal in honor of the Goddess and God. Those present discuss topics related to spirituality and magick in a roundtable style.

The feast begins immediately after the rituals of the Great Days and full moons. It is a sacred extension of the rituals. Feasting, like toasting, is a way of expressing your special relationship and rapport with the Goddess and God, and a way of bringing together the Tuatha or family, both those incarnated here on Earth and those in other dimensions. Even when practicing solitary, prepare a special meal just for yourself.

The following are basic guidelines for the feast that can be used when working with your partner, family, group, or college:

1. Everyone in the ritual brings something to share during the feast, such as food, music, a poem, new divination tool, and so forth.

2. While feasting, toast the Goddesses and Gods by calling out their names, asking them into your circle, and showing them your love and respect.

3. Feasting is a time to promote your spiritual growth and magickal skill, so discuss the art and craft, metaphysics, and the Concept of Oneness.

I find the feast to be the perfect opportunity for sharing Goddess and God dreams and visitations, insights, synchronicities, and messages. When learning the craft, I used the feasts to practice merging, and always asked lots of questions, particularly regarding magickal patterning.

Now I usually do rituals and feasts with my family, but sometimes I enjoy doing rituals with small groups or large gatherings of people because these larger feasts are often times of telling stories, singing songs, drumming, and playing music together.

One game I like to play is called the talking wand, where each member of the group, one by one, takes the altar wand in their hand, and then merging with it, says whatever comes into their minds. If everyone merges deeply enough, this exercise can open many doors.

I encourage you to invent and play craft games for fun and for your own growth. You can devise metaphysical games and work together in pairs or groups, sending healing energy or making talismans.

Closing the Great Circle

At the end of the feast and magick making, thank the Goddess and God for their rapport, kindness, and assistance. Then pull up the Great Circle by holding your athame out in front of you in your power hand, pointed toward the North point. Imagine the blue-white light of the circle being sucked back into the blade as you turn in a 360-degree counterclockwise circle. Take a deep breath, and knock three times on the altar in honor of the Triple Goddess and God. Turn away from your altar. Your ritual is now complete.

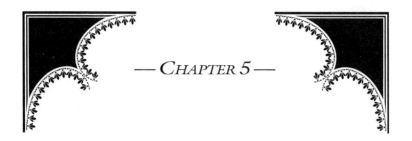

CHAPTER 5

THE WHEEL
OF THE YEAR

The wheel of the year turns sunwise (clockwise), and naturally divides into eight equal-distanced spokes. These spokes mark the eight seasonal festivals called the Great Days. In the Gwyddonic Druid tradition, these quarter and cross-quarter festivals are called Yule, Bridget's Fire, Hertha's Day, Beltane, Letha, Lughnassad, Hellith's Day, and Samhain. Every 45 days, one of the Great Days is celebrated. They remind us of the cycles of nature and of Tarvos Trigaranus's (the Golden One's) progression through the seasons.

Handed down in the tradition, The Story of Esus and Tarvos Trigaranus is a solar myth read aloud on Hertha's Day, Samhain, and also at initiations. This story follows the journey of the sun and sets the stage for the celebration and rituals of the Great Days. The Divine Bull Tarvos, also called the Golden One, symbolizes the sun. The seasonal cycles come about due to the life and death battle between Esus, the hunter God, and Tarvos, the sun. These cycles only continue as a result of the divine intervention of the All Mother.

The threefold principle of birth, life, and death (rebirth) exists within this solar myth, and the cranes with whom Tarvos dances symbolize longevity and cosmic wisdom. They carry with them the blood (DNA blueprint) or essence of the Golden One.

The bull is a key figure in Celtic myth, as the wealth of the Celtic tribes was based on the number of cattle in their possession. Several bull statues and figurines have been found at Celtic archaeological sites, including Hallstatt. The bull, cranes, hunter God, and tree are primary elements of Western magickal traditions. Altars to the hunter God, Esus, whose name is remarkably similar to Jesus, existed at least three centuries before Christianity spread westward. The bull, three cranes, and cutting of the tree all relate to rebirth and a prophetic ceremony in ancient Ireland, in which Druids entered a sacred sleep for the purpose of attaining a vision of the future king. These images appear on a Romano-Celtic carving found in Paris that carries the inscription "Tarvos Trigaranos," meaning the bull with three cranes. The scene on the carving shows the God Esus cutting down a willow tree. A similar carved relief from Trier shows a man cutting down a willow tree, and in the branches of the tree are the head of a bull and three cranes. Here is the story as it was told to me.

The Story of Esus and Tarvos Trigaranus

Long ago when the world was young, a marvelous and wonderful thing happened. In the early Spring, near the pool of the Goddess Coventina, a bull calf was born into the world. At a glance you could see that he was not an ordinary bull calf. His coat shined golden-red and his form was perfect. His eyes were the eyes of the sun.

The golden bull was running about and playing, when out of the air descended three stately cranes. They danced around him in a sunwise circle, and he suddenly, very solemnly, bowed his head to them three times.

As Spring wore on into early Summer, he grew exceedingly fast and soon he was fully grown. Never was there a bull like him, and his fame spread far and wide. Animals, women, children, men, and Gods came to look upon his great beauty. But wonder of wonders, wherever he went, the three cranes also went. They were his constant companions.

His days were filled with endless enjoyment, and the world was full of flowers. For in that ancient time, the world had never known Winter.

Now Esus, the Hunter God, had been roaming through the fields and forests of the world looking for an animal worthy of his appetite, but he found no animal to his satisfaction.

Early one beautiful morning, he happened upon the meadow where he saw the bull and three cranes. One glance at the bull, and Esus knew that his search had ended.

He drew his mighty blade and came upon the sleeping bull, but the cranes saw the danger and gave out a cry of alarm!

The bull rose to do battle with Esus and his golden horns were formidable weapons. The God and the divine bull clashed in combat.

They fought all day and all night, but neither could seem to best the other. The contest continued in this way for many days. It was on a night in the dark of the moon when the bull at last began to fail in strength. There under a great willow, Esus struck the divine bull a final deadly blow.

His blood poured out upon the roots of the willow tree and its leaves turned golden-red at that very instant for pure sorrow and grief.

The cranes made a great crying sound. One of them flew forward, and in a small bowl caught up some of the bull's blood. The three cranes departed, flying toward the South.

An ominous gloom descended upon the Earth. The flowers wilted and the trees dropped their leaves. The sun withdrew his warmth. The world grew cold, and snow fell for the first time.

All humankind prayed to the All Mother to bring back the warmth, or all would perish. She heard and took pity upon nature.

The three cranes came flying back from the South, with one still holding the bowl. It flew to the willow tree where the divine bull had been slain and poured the blood upon the Earth. Suddenly, out of the dust sprang the bull calf, reborn from Mother Earth!

All nature rejoiced. Grass and flowers sprang up. The leaves budded out on the trees. Thus, Spring came again to the world.

But the Hunter God, Esus, heard of the bull's rebirth and sought him out. This was the beginning of the cycle that even to this day persists. Esus ever overcomes the divine bull, but Mother Earth ever causes him to be reborn. Let us pray that the Great Mother will ever cause his rebirth, and may we also, forever be reborn.

The story of Esus and Tarvos is a symbolic representation of the path of the sun as it moves through the yearly cycle. Tarvos is the symbol of life, reborn each year from the seeds of the previous year. Tarvos is stalked by Esus the Hunter, who is symbolic of the death that stalks all life. Tarvos, accompanied by the grey cranes, which are representative of the Threefold Goddess, moves from birth to a pinnacle of vitality and life. At this point, he is slain by the hunter, which symbolizes the harvest and the forces of death, but his blood is gathered up by the three grey cranes. With the help of the Goddess, the blood becomes the blood of life, the seed for the renewal of the life cycle.

On one hand, the story is simple in its description of the life cycle, but on the other hand, the underlying concept, that in life there is death and in death there is renewal, is on many levels profound and lies at the core of Celtic spirituality. Every pattern in life has the three faces of birth, life, and death (rebirth), which is at the heart of the evolution and progression of humanity, both secular and spiritual. For the Celts, the Goddess was the embodiment of these three faces, and it was she who watched over the cycles of nature and the universe.

The Eight Great Days

Feel free to celebrate the Great Days in your own unique way. The rituals below are the edited versions of those given to me. Some say these rituals are more than 250 years old. You can use them word for word, or as a guideline for writing your own rituals.

When doing ritual, keep the season and occasion in mind. Use your intuition and good judgment. Rituals are a divine celebration, so be sure to invite the Goddess and God into your circle and feast! I also suggest trying these rituals during the day. For instance, the Beltane ritual can be very powerful at dawn, when the sun is just coming up. Rituals can be done with a group, a partner, or alone.

Yule - Winter Solstice, 00.00 Degrees Capricorn

The first and last Great Day in the Gwyddonic Druid Tradition is Yule. Celebrated on the eve of the Winter Solstice, the Yule ritual starts just before midnight. Honoring the return of the sun (son) and the symbolic rebirth of Tarvos, a live evergreen tree is decorated with lights. A woman representing the Goddess, and all of her faces of Maid, Mother, and Crone, plugs the lights in, illuminating the tree at the end of the Yule ritual. Plant the live tree the next morning.

The Yule Log, coming either from the householder's land or from a friend, is traditionally burned on this night. The log is treated with respect, decorated in greenery, glitter, and doused in cider and ale. Wheat or corn flour is sprinkled on the log, and then it is burned during the ritual. A piece of the Yule Log is often placed in a safe place on the mantle until next Yule. This protects the home and family, and also attracts abundance for the coming year.

Yule is considered the time to release and resolve any negative feelings you may have toward yourself and others. It is a time to learn from your past mistakes and move forward. One Druid custom is to write the thing you would most like to get rid of in your life on a piece of paper. Take the paper and slowly tear it up, throwing the pieces of paper into the Yule fire with the intention of ridding yourself of the burden.

Suggested Yule altar decorations are holly, ivy, mistletoe, red poinsettias, fir and pine boughs, and cones.

Yule Ritual

Begin the ritual just before midnight, with the shout of "Our Bright Lord returns to us! Hail Kernunnos!" sounding about three minutes after midnight.

High Priestess: Woe to us!
Our Bright Lord is slain.
The Golden Bull lies in the Earth.

Members: Woe to us!

High Priestess: Woe to us!
Our Lord Kernunnos sleeps
In the Earth.
Who hath slain
The Lord of the Fields?

Members: Woe to us!
Lord Esus hath done this.
He hath spilt
The blood of the Divine Bull.
Yea, Lord Esus hath done this!

High Priestess: Oh Lady of Brightness!
Oh Greatest Mother!
Mother of All Things
Hear our plea!

Members: Hear this our plea!

High Priestess: Great Kerridwen
Smile upon us all.
Raise up our Bright Lord again
From out of the dust.
Return the Golden Bull unto us.
Let His Divine Light
Shine upon us again.
Let not the Dark
Have sway over us!

Members: Let not the Dark
                   Have sway over us!

The High Priestess assumes the Goddess position and speaks forth as

The Goddess: I, Kerridwen the Bright
                   Have heard your plea.
                   I shall return
                   Your Lord unto you!

Allow about 30 seconds to elapse after the Goddess speaks and then turn the tree lights on. If the tree is decorated with candles, three women should be selected representing the Maiden, Mother, and Crone, to light the candles with solemn care. As soon as the lights are lit, a member with a strong and clear voice calls forth:

                   Our Bright Lord
                   Returns to us!
                   Hail Kernunnos!

All Members: Hail Kernunnos!
                   Hail Kerridwen!
                   Praise be
                   To our Lord and Lady!

Great merriment and happiness now breaks forth and a circle dance ensues. While dancing, the names of the God and Goddess are chanted louder and louder, over and over, faster and faster:

                   Ker-nun-nos!
                   Ker-rid-wen!

Exchange Yule gifts as symbols of love and renewal. The Yule Feast follows.

Bridget's Fire - 15.00 Degrees Aquarius

The sun Goddess and patroness of the hearth and home, poets, artisans, craftspersons, and smiths is honored in this ritual. Bridget is the sacred bride, and her temple is the sanctuary of the divine need-fire, representing the fire of the sun.

Following this tradition, allow your hearth fire to completely die out on Bridget's Eve. The next morning, build the fire with special care. Take nine (or seven) small twigs, traditionally from different kinds of trees, and light the twigs. Then light the fire with the ignited twigs while chanting three times,

> Bridget, Bridget, Bridget, brightest flame!
> Bridget, Bridget, Bridget, sacred name!

This tradition stems from ancient times when Celtic households let their hearth fires die out on Bridget's Eve. The next morning, the women of the households went to Bridget's temple, lit a branch from the need-fire, and took it home to light their hearth fires.

Another Bridget's Fire custom is to plant a fruit tree. On Bridget's Eve, just before the ritual, a family member waits outside the front door, fruit tree in hand. She or he then knocks loudly on the door three times. Through the closed door, the family members inside the house loudly say together,

> "Bridget, Bridget, Bridget, come into my house!
> Come into my house tonight!
> Open the door for Bridget
> And let Bridget come in!"

Then someone inside the house opens the door with gusto, and the person outside the house brings the fruit tree inside for the evening. Place the tree on the altar, and pamper it. As you plant the tree the next morning, dedicate it to Bridget by chanting her name.

Bridget's Fire Ritual

High Priestess:
Come, let us worship
Our Lady of the Sacred Fire.
Hear us Oh Great Bridget!
We come to ask of you a gift.
For when we receive of Thee
This Divine gift, we receive of Thee
Many goodly Blessings also.
Oh Great Bridget!
Grant us this gift.

Members:
Beloved Mother! Grant us this gift!
Bridget! Bridget! Bridget!
Brightest Flame!
Bridget! Bridget! Bridget!
Sacred Name!

High Priestess:
Oh Bridget, Thou art indeed
Our Mother! Thou art our example.
Perfect Mother! Perfect Wife!
Perfect Lover! (Leman)
Perfect in compassion and understanding.
Lady of Wisdom!
We come to ask of You a gift!

Members:
Beloved Mother! Grant us this gift!
Bridget! Bridget! Bridget!
Brightest Flame!
Bridget! Bridget! Bridget!
Sacred Name!

High Priestess:
Great Goddess!
Thou art every Mother and every Mother
    art Thou!
Thou art every Wife and every
    Wife art Thou!

Thou art every Lover and every
   Lover art Thou!
Thou who art All Mother and All Love;
Grant us this gift!

Members: Beloved Mother! Grant us this gift!
Bridget! Bridget! Bridget!
Brightest Flame!
Bridget! Bridget! Bridget!
Sacred Name!

The Goddess speaks:
Beloved Children!
I, Bridget, hear thy plea!
What wilt Thou
From Me?

All Members: Beloved Mother!
We ask the gift of Thy Presence
in our homes and hearts.
Bridget! Bridget! Bridget!
Brightest Flame!
Bridget! Bridget! Bridget!
Sacred Name!

The Goddess: I come!

At this point in time, a fire is lit and if it has been properly lit, it will blaze up immediately.

The Members *(with great joy and happiness all shout together)*:
Beloved Mother!
We praise Thee!
We thank Thee!
The feast follows.

Hertha's Day (Lady's Day) - Spring Equinox, 00.00 Degrees Aries

When night and day are of equal length, Tarvos, the Golden One, is born near Coventina's Well. Tarvos represents the sun and the well the womb of the Great Earth Mother, Hertha. This ritual honors the sacred birth. Flowers blossom and birds begin nesting to herald the beginning of Spring.

It is the custom to plant Spring flowers and seeds on this day in honor of the Earth Mother Hertha. You can also decorate your altar with living flowers, planting them the next morning in honor of Hertha. Eggs are also decorated with symbols of the Goddess. They are hidden or rolled down hillsides, and then eaten by those engaged in the Spring planting. The following group-style poem is traditionally read on Hertha's Day, always with great drama and gusto!

Poem of the Seasons

Leader:
I shall go as a wren in spring
With sorrow and sighing on silent wing,
And I shall go in our Lady's name,
Aye, till I come home again!

Group:
We shall follow as falcons grey,
And hunt thee cruelly as our prey,
But we shall go in our Master's name,
Aye, to fetch thee home again!

Leader:
Then I shall go as a mouse in May
In fields by night, and cellars by day,
And I shall go in our Lady's name,
Aye, till I come home again!

Group:
And we shall go as black tom cats,
And chase thee through the corn and vats,

	But we shall go in our Master's name, Aye, to fetch thee home again!
Leader:	Then I shall go as an autumn hare, With sorrow and sighing and mickle care, And I shall go in our Lady's name, Aye, till I come home again!
Group:	But we shall follow as swift greyhounds, And dog thy tracks by leaps and bounds, And we shall go in our Master's name, Aye, to fetch thee home again!
Leader:	Then I shall go as a winter trout, With sorrow and sighing and mickle doubt, And I shall go in our Lady's name, Aye, till I come home again!
Group:	But we shall follow as otters swift, And snare thee fast ere thou canst shift, And we shall go in our Master's name, Aye, to fetch thee home again!

Hertha's Day Ritual

High Priestess:	Bright is the day. Sweet is the morning The world waits With hushed breath For this wondrous event That is now a'coming.
Members:	Tell us! Tell us! Pray do! Tell us! Tell us! We Pray you! What event?! What portent?!

High Priestess: Birds of every kind
Animals large and small
More than I can tell
Gather there, see them all
At Coventina's Well
To see this wondrous thing
that is now a'coming.

Members: Tell us! Tell us!
Pray do!
Tell us! Tell us!
We Pray you!
What event?!
What portent?!

High Priestess: See the sweet Mother
How brave She is!
Her sighs are carried
On the wind
And touch the hearts
of every creature.
(pause)
Oh! Her Blessed Son is born!
All Nature breaks forth in joy.
The birds of every kind
Sing their sweetest songs
For our Lord is born!
The Golden One is born!

Members: Oh blessed event!
Our Lord is born!
The Golden One is born!

High Priestess: Look now!
Look upon a strange thing!
Three Grey Cranes

Have flown down.
Three Grey Cranes
Stately and tall
Dance about
Our Blessed Lord
So sweet and small.

Members: Three Grey Cranes
Dancing
What a sight!
Three Grey Cranes
Dancing
In the Sun's Light.

High Priestess: The Three bow to the Mother
They bow to the Son
The Mother bows to the Three
And so does her Beloved One.

Members: Three Grey Cranes
Bowing
What a sight!
Three Grey Cranes
Bowing
In the Sun's Light.

High Priestess: Come, let us dance
Let us sing and bow
Bow to the Mother
Bow to the Son
Bow to the Three
I bow to you
And you bow to me.

Members: We bow to the Mother
We bow to the Son
We bow to the Three

	You bow to us We bow to thee!
All:	We bow to the Mother We bow to the Son We bow to the Three You bow to us We bow to thee!
	Blessed Be!!!

The feast may follow.

Beltane, The Adventure of the Sun (May Day) - 15.00 Degrees Taurus

On Beltane Eve, natural sexual energies are at their peak. It is interesting to note that many historic events took place on Beltane, for instance, the coming of the Tuatha De Danann. Beltane marks the bright part of the year and a time of natural balance.

On May Day, the May Queen and King represent the Goddess and God and the sacred marriage of the Earth and sky. They dance around the red and white May Pole, in honor of springtime greening. They symbolize the female and male powers of fertility, creation, and regeneration. In past times, couples would make love in the fields to ensure a good harvest. Bonfires at Beltane honor the great fire and source of all life, the sun. Leaping over the sacred fire purifies and protects you. You can also use a large candle to do this, setting it on the floor, and carefully leaping over it.

An abundant harvest and fair weather for the season can be had by walking around a sacred place, well, tree, or stone in a sunwise direction three times, while chanting the names of the Goddess and God. For good luck, you can rise and watch the sunrise from a hilltop. Suggested altar decorations are herbs, boughs, hawthorn flowers, and roses. The following is a traditional fertility song that is sung on Beltane morning:

We've been rambling all the night,
And sometime of this day,
And turning back again,
We bring a garland gay.
A garland gay we bring you here,
And at your door we stand,
It is a sprout well budded out,
The work of our Lady's hand.

Beltane Ritual

High Priestess: Behold! He cometh!
Out of the East He comes!
His face with glory
Shines upon the Earth. (*pause*)

Behold! He cometh!
Our Bright Lord
In joyful mood
Prancing!
Dancing!
Out of the East He comes!

Members: Prancing!
Dancing!
Out of the East He comes!

High Priestess: The wind whispers:
Kernunnos.
Lord Kernunnos.
Kernunnos.

The birds sing:
Tarvos!
Golden Bull!
Tarvos!
The animals call:
Golden One!
Kernunnos!
Golden One!
And all say:
Behold! He cometh
Out of the East He comes
Prancing!
Dancing!

Members:

Prancing!
Dancing!
Out of the East He comes!
Ayea!
He comes!

High Priestess:

Our Bright Lord
Looks upon all with kindest love.
He knows no sorrow nor wishes any.
The Three Grey Cranes
Love our Lord
They know all sorrow
but They wish none
So...They dance!

So dance now
While you may
The seasons turn
Now is the time
To joyfully play!
Away! Away! Away!

The High Priestess takes a man by the hand, and he takes a woman by the hand, and she takes a man by the hand, and so on, until everyone is in a line. Then the High Priestess leads a follow-the-leader dance around the area. Do this playfully for five or ten minutes. The High Priestess returns to her original position before the altar when the dance is done.

High Priestess: May the joy
                        Of our Golden Lord
                        Be upon you!

Members: And you also, Lady!

The feast follows.

Letha (Midsummer) - Summer Solstice, 00.00 Degrees Cancer

On the longest day of the year, the Golden One, the sun, is at its zenith. It is a time of balance between the powers of light and dark. Lugh, the Celtic God identified with the moon, rules the six-month period from Letha to Yule, when the days grow shorter. Letha means "death," as in dying light of the sun. The nights become longer and the light of the moon becomes more powerful.

Lavender can be burned in your censer (or bonfire) as an offering to the Goddess and God on Midsummer's Eve. Suggested altar decorations include apples, feathers, and seasonal flowers. You can also decorate trees near wells with flowers or white feathers, or put colored stones in fountains and pools. Direct your prayers for abundance and prosperity to Anu, the Celtic Mother Goddess.

Midsummer's Eve Ritual

High Priestess: Dancing and Prancing
Our Bright Lord comes
The Lord of Light
Comes from the East!

Members: Dancing and Prancing
He comes from the East!

High Priestess: On His way
On a summer's day
He meets a Lovely Lady
Dressed in Silver,
Dressed in Grey.

Members: Who is this Lady
Tell us, pray
Dressed in Silver
Dressed in Grey?!

High Priestess: Do you not know Her?
You have all seen Her
At least once before
And will again
When She, with sweetest smile
Bids you to sleep awhile
To rest awhile
in Her land. *(pause)*

She is Rhiannon
Lady of Avalon
Lady of the Golden Apples
Lady of Rest
In the Land of the Blest. *(pause)*

She meets our Lord
On Her arm
In a basket
Are 12 Golden Apples.

Our Bright Lord
is right glad
When She gives
Him One to eat.

He eats it
And it is most sweet
But it seems there is
A coldness in His feet.

With a smile
She gives Him another
and it tastes sweeter still
But a coldness
Seems to numb His will.

She gives Him another
And it tastes so good
But the coldness was so great
That when She offered Him another
He could not eat it
If He would!

Then She, with a smile said,
"Nine months of each year,
The world has nought to fear.
For You shall be
Here for all to see.
But three months
You shall stay with Me
In the Land of Avalon
Among the Dead!"

> Our Lord hung His head
> But a sweet smile
> Came over His face
> He began to Dance
> And He began to Prance
> And ever at a faster pace!

All:
> Let us Dance!
> And Prance!
> While we may
> For time flees away!

(All dance a sunwise Circle Dance.)

The feast follows.

Lughnassad (Lugh's Wedding Feast) - 15.00 Degrees Leo

Held just after sunset on the eve of the Great Day, this first fruits harvest ritual honors the wedding of the Celtic rose mother, Rosemerta to Lugh, the Celtic lord of the night. This is a particularly auspicious time for weddings as Lughnassad represents the marriage of the powers of light and darkness, the sun and moon, and life and death. It marks the sun's descent, and it's consummate union with the Earth Mother. When the Goddess marries the Lugh, she marries death, and in doing so, receives many wonderful and sacred gifts.

Decorate your altar with berries, flowers, corn, and all kinds of vegetables. Make oat cakes and share them with friends during the Lughnassad feast, or make a simple corn dolly from corn husks and ribbon. Put the dolly in the kitchen for a year and a day to protect and bless your home.

Lughnassad Ritual

High Priest: Hear ye! Hear ye!

Come one and all
Tonight is the Wedding
Of Lugh our Lord.

Members: We come! We come!
But what shall we bring?!

High Priest: Bring yourselves
And a merry heart!
For it will be merry meet
And merry part!

Come ye and honor
Our Lord and Lady
At this celebration,
Their Wedding Feast!

Members: We come!
For we are honored
To attend the Wedding Feast
Of our Lord and Lady!
But pray, sir!
Say a word
About our Lord and Lady!

High Priest: That I will!
First I will speak
Of our Loving Lady!

Her beauty is the
Beauty that makes
Every thing beautiful.
There is none to equal it!

She is the Love
That every man longs for.
She is the mate
That every man desires!
She is our most desired
In every way!

It was our Lady
Who taught us to Weave
And taught us
Every gentle Craft
That eases the burden
Of hardihood.

It was our Great Lady
Who gave us Fire
That we might
Warm our hearths and homes.

This is the word
I speak for yours
And my Dear Lady!

Members: You said it well!
How about a word
About our Lord!

High Priest: Master of All Arts!
He is Lugh of the Living Lance
The mighty Far-Shooter.

Of lovers, Lugh is the best!
The handsome Long Handed One
Is a Master with his
Rod-sling and magic spear.

Of carpenters, Lugh is the best!
Of smiths, Lugh is the best!
Of bronze workers, Lugh is the best!
Of harpists, Lugh is the best!
Of chess players, Lugh is the best!
Of warriors, Lugh is the best!

Tale-teller of ancestors
Lugh made poetry
The Magic Art it is.
Masterful physician
If it had not been for Lugh
Singing would not heal!

It is the light of the long hand
Sun God of crowning glory
Who sits upon the sage's seat
The place of the wisest One.

This is the word
I speak for yours
And my Great Lord!

Members: You said it well!
For we are honored
To attend the Wedding Feast
Of our Lord and Lady!

With Perfect Peace
And Perfect Love
We bring ourselves
And a merry heart!

For it will be merry meet
And merry part!

The feast follows.

Hellith's Day - Autumnal Equinox, 00.00 Degrees Libra

Hellith is the Celtic God of the dying sun. The ancient Druids did not see "Hell" or "Hel" as a place of punishment like the Christians do, but rather an Otherworldly place you went to when you died of old age or disease.

This ritual begins just after sunset on the eve of the autumnal equinox. It is a magickal night, a time for gathering together at the final harvest and of finishing the old business of Summer. Hellith's Day is also a time for collecting seeds for the coming year. Everyone shares activities, such as the destruction of the barley (or corn) mother. Everyone tells stories, plays music, and toasts the deities. You can also offer a libation of apple cider or wine to a tree on this day.

Suggestions for altar decorations are cornucopias, acorns, breads, cakes, and fruits of the last harvest. Set your altar table with your best finery, and feast upon the finest foods on this Great Day. As an offering of thanks and to bring good fortune and long life, you can make a small outdoor shrine for the faeries and elementals. Do this just before sunset on Hellith's Eve, and use only flowers and vegetables free from blemish or blight.

Hellith's Day Ritual

High Priestess: There is the sound
Of baying Hounds
Coming over the hills
From far away
A cold fear
Grips my heart.

Members: We feel it, too
The same as you!
What does this mean?
Tell us, we pray you!

High Priestess: See the Golden Bull
As He goes
Dancing
Prancing?

See the Three Grey Cranes
Each of Them knows
As They go
Dancing
Prancing
The Answer!

But our Bright Lord
Has a will to live.
He is full
Of the Love of Life
Though He hears
The Hounds of Death
That Bay,
He has a will to live
And will be full of joy
While He May.

All: Then, let us as the samewise do
Come Dance with us
And we'll Dance with you!

Now then!
Come Dance with us
And we'll Dance with you!

As soon as these words are spoken, begin to dance with each other very slowly and carefully, making each step last. Don't make a sound. Do this until the energy and intensity builds, and then begin making sounds like Hounds baying after their prey. Afterward, relax and drink water and juice before you eat the feast. You need to be lighthearted by the time you eat.

The feast follows.

Samhain (Halloween) - 15.00 Degrees Scorpio

Celebrated after sunset, Samhain means "Summer's end." It marks the dark half of the year, ruled by the dark Goddess and her consort. It is a time of death, but also of rebirth, which is symbolized by the sprig of holly in the Samhain Ritual.

The veils between worlds draw to their thinnest on Samhain Eve, and time and space become fluid. The doorways to the Otherworld are thrown open and the spirits of the Otherworld can communicate with mortals. This is one of the best times for contact experiences with the Goddess and God.

The Oracle of Death is a traditional Samhain practice. Those present draw lots to decide who acts as the Oracle. The person selected sits in a dark, quiet corner and answers questions about the future. The idea is that Death already knows the answer.

Another Samhain custom is the Dumb Supper. A feast for the spirits in the land such as ancestors, deities, faeries, and elementals, plates are filled with food and drink and put outside on the doorstep at night. Three red candles are placed around the plates, and then lit and allowed to safely burn down during the night. Any food or drink that remains in the morning is put into the Earth and given to the Goddess.

To the Celtic Druids, the spirit of a person resided in the head, hence the concept of the sacred head. The jack-o-lantern symbolizes this concept. The lit candle inside the jack-o-lantern represents the living spirit or "awen."

Samhain Ritual

High Priestess: See, Behold our stately Lord
As He frolics in the meadows.
He is full of joy
And the Love of Life.
See! Behold the Three Grey Cranes
As They Dance about Him.
They are full of Love for Him.
The Three Grey Ladies.
See! Behold the world
Is full of gladness.
They live in the joy
Of our Great Lord. *(pause)*

(Suddenly) Woe! Woe! Oh Woe!

Members: What betides thee, Lady?!
Why do you moan?

High Priestess: See! Behold Lord Esus!
Greatest Hunter!
Lord of Hunters!
He has espied
The Noblest of Prey
And will not stop
Until Him, He shall slay.

Members:	Woe! Woe! Oh Woe! Woe hath befallen us!
High Priestess:	See! Behold the two Noblest of Lords Do in combat lock The Three Grey Cranes weep to the Highest Gods To save Their Lord Oh woe to us! The whole world groans.
Members:	Woe! Woe! Oh Woe! Woe hath befallen us!
High Priestess:	With one great stroke, Lord Esus fells our Divine Lord. His blood stains the Earth and All Nature shudders. He raises His mighty head and Looks on Life for the last time With Loving eyes. And with a stately sigh Then down His head He doth die. He hath gone to the Land Of the Queen of those who die.
Members:	Woe to us! He hath gone down to The Land of Death!
High Priestess:	Oh Great Mother! Kerridwen the Blessed! Give us a sign That our Beloved Lord Will return to us.

Mother of Mothers
Show us a Sign
Or we shall perish.

Members: Kerridwen the Blessed
Show us a Sign!

The High Priestess or some worthy woman may play the part of the Goddess.

The Goddess Speaks:

Behold! My children,
I have heard your plea.
Her is your Sign from Me!

She holds forth a fresh sprig of greenery, traditionally a sprig of holly with red berries.

All: Praise be to You, Greatest Goddess!
We have seen Thy Sign
And know its deepest meaning!
Blessed Be!

The feast follows.

The 13 Druid Moons

The moon holds a fascination for most people. As human beings, we consist of mostly water. The moon affects the flow of water on the Earth, and thus our bodies. One way to see the moon is in the three stages of maid, mother, and crone. The new or waxing moon is the maid, the virgin adolescent, full of curiosity, hope, and desire. The mother is the exquisite full moon, the divine lady in all her magnificence. The crone is the dark of the moon. Powerful and wise, she has knowledge because she has lived so long and has had so many different experiences.

You can pinpoint the exact time of the full or high moon using a good calendar or a basic ephemeris available at bookstores. It is customary to celebrate the full moon on the night closest to the actual full moon, preferably during the exact time the moon is full or while the moon is still waxing. This is when the power is the strongest for doing positive magick!

There are 13 high moons in the Gwyddonic Druid tradition. Beginning with the first full moon after Yule, their names represent the seasonal cycle of the year: 1) Wolf, 2) Storm, 3) Chaste, 4) Seed, 5) Hare, 6) Dyad, 7) Mead, 8) Wort, 9) Barley, 10) Wine, 11) Blood, 12) Snow, and 13) Oak.

Ritual of the Boon Moon

Do this ritual on the sixth full moon after Yule. A woman designated as the High Priestess is the Goddess for the duration of this ritual. She sits in a candle-lit room alone, and the group members go into the room, one at a time. The order of members into the room can be decided by picking cards from a tarot deck. The highest card goes first.

The woman acting as the Goddess goes through the boon ritual separately with each member. In the privacy of the boon room, she grants each person a secret boon as a reward for their good works over the past year. She may also lay a woe on any member who hasn't done any good works or has brought disrepute upon the art and craft. When working solitary, you can improvise and ask a favorite Goddess such as Kerridwen, Anu, or Bridget, for your boon.

Over the years I have done this ritual with many people, and it is always incredibly powerful. When done properly, the boon room becomes like an Otherworld. The air seems to ripple and sparkle with divine energy. When kneeling before the Goddess, people often lose their balance or start shaking. This is a natural reaction to the intense energy generated by the boon ritual.

Your boon can be anything you deeply desire. For example, you can ask for dramatically increased creativity over the next year, or a better job, or for more love and romance in your life. Unlike many other spiritual paths, in the Celtic Druid tradition you directly petition the Goddess and God and ask for exactly what you want. Then you take the steps to make sure your boon comes true and sings out with divine power! Here are the complete instructions for the ritual of granting a boon:

1. Set up a separate altar in a separate room. Light the candles and incense, and then dim the lights, or better yet, turn them off.

2. The woman designated as the Goddess uses her athame to draw a circle of light around the room. She cuts an energetic door where the physical doorway is, so others in the group can come and go. She calls in the four wards, stands or sits next to the altar, and waits for the first person to enter the room.

3. The first group member, the one who picked the highest card, enters the room, steps through the energetic gate, and then closes both doors, the physical and energetic. The member goes before the Goddess and kneels down.

4. The Goddess asks, "What is thy name?"

5. The member gives a false name. "I am [False Name]."

6. The Goddess asks again, this time a little more loudly. "What is thy name?!"

7. The member gives a second false name. "I am [False Name]."

8. The Goddess asks a third time, her voice a little louder and more demanding, "What is thy name?!!"

9. The member gives her or his true craft name. "I am [True Name]."

10. The Goddess addresses the member, "[True Name], I know thee and know thee full well, for I have seen thy comings and goings. [True Name], what dost thou seek?"

11. The member says, "Great One I pray that Thou will grant me a boon."

12. The Goddess says, "[True Name], I have said that I know thee well and have seen thy comings and goings. I have seen thy good works (or bad works)." The Goddess may then tell of one of the good or bad works of the member. If it is a good work, the Goddess says, "I will grant thy boon! What wilt thou?"

13. The members says, "I pray Great One, Thou will grant me this boon: [The member tells what it is she or he desires, for example, a better job, true love, improved health].

14. When the member who has performed good works has asked for his boon, the Goddess says, "[True Name], I grant it to thee!"

15. The member says, "Praise be to Thee! Blessed be! Blessed be! Blessed be!" bowing on each "Blessed be," continually facing the Goddess as she or he backs out of the room and departs with gladness.

16. If the Goddess tells of a bad work, she says, "I will not grant thy boon, but on thee I lay this woe: [She then names some task that the member must perform for the benefit of someone else].

17. The member replies, "Though the woe lays heavy on me, I know it will be to my good. Blessed be! Blessed be! Blessed be!" The member bows with each "blessed be" and then backs out of the room.

Full Moon Circle Magick

Energy forms the foundation of each healing work. Everything is energy. Healing involves gathering positive energy and directing it through expectation, desire, and merging, into reality. The strength of your rapport with the Goddess and God, and the depth of your merge with Oneness, powers your healing ability.

When doing healing works, be aware of your intent and also consider the timeliness of the work. Each of the 13 moons has a different harmonic of energy that can be applied for specific healing work. For example, the Chaste Moon sets the stage for personal purification and releasing old habits, whereas the Blood Moon is best for healing blood circulation problems.

Following is the number, name, and qualities, of the 13 moons:

1: Wolf Moon — Unity, Oneness, teamwork, and group efforts.

2: Storm Moon — Duality and polarity; as above, so below.

3: Chaste Moon — The Triple Goddess of Maid, Mother, and Crone.

4: Seed Moon — The solidity of the four elements of manifestation. Planting seeds of the future.

5: Hare Moon — Control of the self, the physical manifestation, personal awareness.

6: Dyad Moon — Time, lifetimes, and boons.

7: Mead Moon — Lunar fertility, lucid dreams, sex magic.

8: Wort Moon — The yearly cycle, purification, healing, brewing, and baking.

9: Barley Moon — Wisdom, knowledge, and finishing business.

10: Wine Moon — Prophecy and creative genius.

11: Blood Moon — Ancestry, fecundity, and maternity.

12: Snow Moon — Divine connection and purpose.

13: Oak Moon — Rebirth, new beginnings, shape shifting, and transmigration.

Flowing with the full moon's energy, healing work uses the directions and their corresponding Elements. North (Earth) gives you a foundation from which to work. East (Air) grants you freedom of movement and mental agility, while South (Fire) gives you strength and power. West (Water) shows you how to get in touch with your intuitive powers and flow. All directions are represented by spirit. When you are tapped into spirit, into the Goddess and God, into Oneness, is when your healing ability is most powerful.

Ritual of a Full Moon Circle Magick

The intense power of the full moon circle can be used for healing rituals, manifesting, and expanding your spiritual awareness. Traditionally, High Moon rituals and healings begin after dark. You can play soft instrumental Celtic music to add a little ambiance to the ritual. Follow these steps to do your own full moon healing work. You will find that the power builds within the circle with each step.

1. Set your altar with your tools. Light the incense and candle(s). Take a few moments to enjoy the scent of the incense and to watch the candle flame.

2. Clear out your magickal space and neutralize any negative energies with cobalt-blue light, saying, "May all evil and foulness be gone from this place. I ask this in the Lady's name. Be gone, now and forever more." Do this three times, turning in a clockwise circle, and sweeping the area with your hands and mind.

3. Next, draw a clockwise circle around your magickal space with your athame, seeing the blue-white flame flaring out of the blade's tip.

4. Purify the four corners with salt, starting at the North point and continuing around the circle to the East, South, and West points. At each point, chant, "Ayea, Ayea Kerridwen!, Ayea, Ayea Kernunnos!, Ayea, Ayea, Ayea!"

5. Face the altar, after moving around the four corners of the circle, and say in a firm voice, "Blessed be! Blessed be the Goddesses and Gods! Blessed be all who are gathered here."

6. Merge with the Goddess and God, with Oneness, and then knock nine times on the altar with the handle of your athame or wand, in three series of three.

7. Use your athame to draw a circle of sacred fire on top of the Great Circle. Do this by visualizing a white flame coming out of the tip of your athame as you lay the circle of white on top of the cobalt blue circle you have already drawn.

8. Call in the four wards.

9. Use your athame to cut an energetic doorway or gate just below the East point of your circle. This is the entryway and exit from the circle. Be sure to close or open this energetic gate with your athame whenever you exit or enter the circle.

10. Stand in the center of the circle or next to your altar. Begin to chant the names of the Goddesses and Gods to bring their divine energy into your circle. Use swaying and dancing to build up the intensity of the chant, and then release the energy when it has reached it's power peak. When you release it, direct it toward a specific goal.

11. Before doing the healing work, examine your intention. What is your expectation? If the person to be healed is present, then that person must desire

to be healed. Ask her or him, "Do you want this healing? Do you accept this healing energy?" Continue with the healing work, only after you receive a strong confirmation from the person that they want to participate fully in the healing. If you meet with a less-than-positive response, stop, and go on to another healing.

12. Select the divine sponsors for the healing work. Select Goddesses and Gods based upon your rapport and their attributes. Every Goddess and consort emits and absorbs certain types of energies, elemental and otherwise. Match these energies as closely as you can to the healing work. For example, if a malady can be remedied by application of warm wet heat, ask Borvo to be one of your sponsors in the healing. Three sponsors are selected for each healing work.

13. Join hands when working with your mate, family, or group. Energy flows more efficiently in an alternating current, so make an effort to link your healing circle in an alternating pattern; boy, girl, boy, girl, and so on.

14. Begin imagining a bright blue light washing out the illness or disease. Use deep breathing and visualization to do this. Visualize, feel, taste, touch and smell the colors of light you use in healing. Be the light. Be the energy of each color.
Continue washing the problem area out with blue light for a minute or longer.

15. Change the blue light to bright green light. Green light sets up a new healthy pattern. Keep visualizing green light penetrating the problem area for a minute or longer.

16. Imagine a bright sun gold light replacing the green light. Gold light fuels the new healthy pattern. Do this for a minute or longer.

17. Begin to chant the names of the sponsors you have chosen. Traditionally the Goddess and God name is chanted three times or nine times. Again use alternating female and male energies in your chanting pattern. For example, if you chose Kerridwen, Dagda, and Bridget to be your sponsors, you would chant, "Kerridwen, Kerridwen, Kerridwen! Dagda, Dagda, Dagda! Bridget, Bridget, Bridget! Ayea, Ayea, Ayea!"

18. Merge deeply with Oneness, and peak the energy within and without you. As you chant the divine names, run your arms out and upward, hands joined. Allow the healing energy to move through you, and outward towards your selected destination. In a firm and focussed voice, chant the final triplet, "Ayea, Ayea, Ayea!," and let go of the hands of those next to you. Release the healing energy and direct it to its destination. If the person is physically present, actually lay your hands on the person and run the healing energy directly into her or him for a couple of minutes. In your heart, know that the healing is complete. Turn your mind to this result.

19. When finished, give your heartfelt thanks to the Goddess and God for their help, healing energy, and blessing. Pull up your circle, knock three times on your altar with the base of your wand in honor of the Triple Goddess, and put everything away.

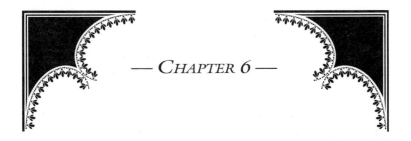

CHAPTER 6

THE FIVE MAGICKAL WORKS

The five magickal works in Gwyddonic Druidism are the talisman, pentacle, binding, healing work, and cone of power. Also called the "Little Works," they are used to attain magickal goals and create positive life patterns. The five works are examples of how to gather, build, and move energy. The talisman shows you how to store positive energy, while the pentacle gives you an opportunity to pattern it. The binding shows you how to purposefully influence your energetic space. The healing work provides ways for influencing the energetic patterns in the body, and the cone of power shows you how to gather and release a large mass of merged energy toward a specific goal.

When doing magick, having positive, clear intentions can help you attain your goals, while negative, chaotic intentions will destroy your goals. Because of this, it is important to stay positive when performing the five magickal works. Upon successfully completing the fifth work by raising a cone of power, you, the seeker, lift another veil. This leads to expanded awareness.

Keep in mind when doing magick that an error in calculation will result in an error in situation. The error can occur in any of the steps of the work. Be absolutely sure that you know what you want, and that you really want it!

The Three Eyes of Kerridwen

Expectation, desire, and merging are the three eyes of Kerridwen. They are built into each of the five magickal works. The secret of success in any magical work can be found within the three eyes. The one-two-three eyes formula for patterning magickal energy is as follows:

1. Have a crystal clear expectation of your magickal goal. Expectation is the nature, qualities, and circumstances of your goal.

2. Build an intensely strong desire toward your expectation. Desire is how much you hope, wish, long, or crave for your goal. The more intensely you want something, the more likely you will get it.

3. Merge with Oneness as deeply as you possibly can, and then a little deeper still, allowing your expectation and desire to flow out of you and circulate into Oneness. When in a merged state of mind, you are aware that you are One with *everything*! Time and space become fluid. Your

ego-awareness diffuses like a cloud dissolving into the air. Merging is a sacred state of awareness, a divine doorway. What you do once you enter the doorway is your responsibility.

All magickal traditions involve gathering, moving, directing, and shaping energy into patterns, with merging as the key for attaining your magickal goals. Through thought and action, you are ultimately responsible for creating your life. This is why it is so important to turn your mind toward your hopes and goals, rather than focusing on your fears and disappointments.

Merging

Merging is an innate ability that all children possess. As adults, we tend to forget this natural talent, but at a moment's notice, we can regain it.

Everyone can experience merging. It is an incredibly pleasant state of awareness, for instance, the feeling you have when you are in love or when you look into the eyes of your newborn baby. Merging is how it feels when you watch the sun set slowly at the beach or when walking in an old growth forest. Merging is that boundless feeling that comes over you when you are in synchronicity and at one with everything. You are connected with the entire web of life.

The deeper you merge, the stronger the magick. When you set out upon the Great Adventure, you learn to merge with the manifested universe—that which already exists. As your magickal awareness expands, you begin to merge with the unmanifested universe, a continuously swirling cauldron of a place where spontaneous creation circumvents "natural law." In this way, merging with Oneness becomes your gateway to creativity and Otherworlds of experience.

The sensations you experience when merging can range from peacefulness, incredible calmness, gentle relaxation, and well-being to spinning, flying, whirling, floating, or intense happiness. Often during merging, you feel like you're floating and sense yourself being both everything and nothing, all at the same time.

Ways of merging deeper include using breathing exercises, staring at candlelight, listening to music, drumming, aromatherapy, and visualization techniques. Liquor and psychoactive drugs also induce merging, but refrain from using them during magick or ritual. Magick is most powerful when you have all of your senses operating at full capacity.

In the Gwyddonic Druid tradition, there are three merges that lead to Godhood and Goddesshood. Each merge must be pure and deep. They are as follows:

1. Merge so deeply with the manifested that you can't find any residue of ego within yourself.

2. Merge so deeply with the unmanifested that you become unaware of any selfness.

3. Merge so deeply that you are one with the manifested and unmanifested, and see that each is truly One, without separation or difference.

Merging is a sort of paradox because you experience unique consciousness while becoming One with all things, while having no apparent consciousness. You diffuse or pass through ordinary reality to a place beyond description, a boundless place of light. When you merge deep enough, it feels like going home.

Positive, Neutral, and Negative Energy

Oneness is made up of energy. This energy has positive, neutral, and negative expressions. Positive energy begets positive outcomes. The positive force creates patterns out of energy and matter. Negative energy creates negative outcomes and causes random factors to arise in energy and matter. I suggest that you gather and direct only positive energy in your rituals, healings, and magickal works. If you do negative magick, it will come back at you and eventually destroy you. The Dark One gives death, while the Bright One gives life.

The time has come to gather together and bring the light and joy back to a land filled with negativity and despair. It is a New Age of humankind, where we can, once again, openly acknowledge and honor the Goddess and God. We can move toward a positive and loving future.

The Order of the Ritual of a Magickal Work

When doing the five magickal works, perform them in order (1 to 5) to ensure that the teachings are as powerful as possible. They are formulated to show you how to collect and transfer energy into an object, as well as how to attract and direct energy into a tangible form. You also learn how to heal energetic systems and how to move energy outward towards specific goals.

Do the works at your own pace. I suggest that you do one work at a time, allowing a few days or weeks between works. You can also repeat the work several times in order to perfect your technique.

Dawn, noon, sunset, twilight, and midnight are the power times. They are the best times of the day to do magickal works. You can also do your works on the eves of the Great Days or on the full moons. Doing so gives them even more magickal power. Once you have completed the five works, it is a time to celebrate. Do something special to mark the occasion!

The Nine Steps of the Ritual of a Magickal Work

1. Set your altar table with your magickal tools and all of the items you need for the magickal work. Light the candle and incense. If you use a special chant, place it where you can easily see the words. Put the images of the Goddess and God on your altar, and direct your gestures and words in their direction.

2. Use your athame to draw a sacred circle or sphere, starting at the North point. Visualize a blue-white flame of energy flowing from the tip of the blade, surrounding you in its sacred and protective fire.

3. Knock nine times, in three sets of three, on the altar surface with base of your wand.

4. Purify your working area by putting water in your craft bowl and then adding three pinches of salt. Take a spring of greenery and dip it in the salted water, and starting at the North point of the circle, lightly sprinkle the circle in a clockwise motion.

5. As you sprinkle the salt water, say:

> Begone from here all darkness and foulness. Begone from this place in Our Lady's Name. Begone now and forevermore!

6. Call divine grace and blessings of the Celtic Goddess and God into your sacred circle. To do this, face the North point of the circle, and say:

> Ayea, Ayea, Kerridwen,
> Ayea, Ayea, Kernunnos!

Face the East point and repeat:

> Ayea, Ayea, Kerridwen,
> Ayea, Ayea, Kernunnos!

Face the South and say:

> Ayea, Ayea, Kerridwen,
> Ayea, Ayea, Kernunnos!

Do the same thing as you face West.

7. Do one magickal work per session in the order they appear, 1 to 5.

8. After each magickal work, thank the Goddess and God for their presence, guidance, and blessings.

9. When you are done with the work, pull up the circle, purify yourself, and put everything away.

The First Magickal Work—
The Talisman

Talismans give power to the owner and are often passed on through generations. Probably the most famous talisman is the Philosopher's Stone. Possession of this touchstone enabled its owner to magickally turn base metals into gold.

A talisman is a magickal object that you energetically encode with specific qualities and feelings, such as the feeling of love. It then radiates these qualities. Usually small and carried or worn on your person, such as jewelry and coins, talismans can be made from any object, but stones and metals are the best choices.

Instructions for Making a Talisman

Use the following 13 steps to make your own talisman:

1. Choose the object you are going to use for your talisman.

2. Decide what feeling or quality you are going to put in it.

3. Determine your talisman's area of influence, for example, two feet, 15 feet, or a mile.

4. Do steps 1 to 6 of the Nine Steps of the Ritual of a Magickal Work.

5. Put two identical white candles in holders, and then place them on your altar and light them.

6. Put the object you are making into a talisman directly in front of you between the two white candles where you can easily see it.

7. Merge, using your emotions, sensation, or whatever works for you, and fill your mind with the feeling or quality you want to place into your talisman.

8. Pick the talisman object up from the altar, and then implant the feeling or quality into your talisman by visualizing a laser beam of light moving

from your forehead and from the palms of your hands and fingertips into the talisman.

9. Use rhythmic breathing to deepen the merge. Breathe in for three counts, still your breath for three counts, and then exhale for three counts.

10. Direct all of your attention, desire, and emotion into the object, and imagine the feeling or quality being absorbed and accepted by the very atoms of your talisman.

11. Imagine the area of the talisman's influence. Do this by imagining it radiating like an egg of energy outward to your specifics.

12. Place the talisman back down between the candles.

13. Clap your hands together, and then leave the area for a few minutes to clear your mind.

Repeat the procedure until you feel satisfied with the results. After completing the talisman, purify yourself and put everything away.

Talisman Visualization

Visualizing something is the first step toward creating an experience of it in your life. When you imagine or visualize something, you move your mind energy toward and focus on what it is you are imagining, and thereby experience, at least on an energetic level, what you are imagining. You not only create the image in your mind, you create an energetic experience of it. In this way, visualization becomes like trying on different clothes. The visualizations that are most appealing to you are the ones you can do again and again for personal empowerment. The most effective way to do visualization is to tape record the visualization, and then play it back just before you go to sleep and just upon waking. These are the times when your mind is most suggestible. But you don't have to limit visualizations to these times. You can do them whenever you need a magickal break from the daily grind.

Whenever doing visualizations, be sure to get as comfortable and relaxed as possible. Take your shoes off and either sit or recline comfortably, and loosen any clothing, belts, or jewelry that are tight or binding. Be sure to turn off the phone so you don't hear the ringer or answering machine. Also, turn off your beeper if you have one. (Put your Furby in another room!) Make certain everyone in your home, including your pets, knows you are not to be disturbed while you are doing your visualizations.

Another powerful way to use visualization is to read a part of the visualization, and then play it out in your head, and then read the next part, and imagine it, and so forth. Do this slowly and savor all of the parts of the visualization. This process results in expanded awareness, and can really fuel your creative efforts.

You will need a stone for this visualization. Clear the stone out by soaking it in salt water for a few minutes or by rinsing it in cool water. Sit or lie back, and hold the stone in your power hand. Get as comfortable as you can, breathing deeply and relaxing your muscles. Breathe in to the count of three, holding your breath for three counts, and then exhale completely. While you are breathing in this way, allow all of the stress and worries of the day to flow out of you each time you exhale.

Imagine you are walking down a path towards a garden. Use your breathing to focus on the garden a little more. Imagine your bare feet touching the soft clover that crowds the edge of the garden path. You walk along until you reach an iron gate, fashioned with spirals, suns, moons, and stars. You peer over the ornate gate, and then touch the cool curving spirals on it. You gently push the gate open and step into the garden. You find yourself in a magickal garden where things drift off time's main road. Flowers of every kind bloom around you, and large, curvaceous ash trees stretch out over your head like beautiful Goddesses. The trees sparkle with beauty and light. You gaze at their splendor with eyes you've not yet used, and you feel a loving, ancient connection.

The trees beckon you, and as you walk towards them, you notice a flash of sky blue light coming from a stone in the center of the path. Reaching down, you pick up a flat stone. Your fingers caress the smooth surface before turning it over and feeling the other side. You feel the division between the surface of the stone and your fingers blur and for a moment you become the stone, and the stone becomes you.

While still stroking the stone, you move to a place in the center of the ash trees, where there is a small pool. You sit down next to the pool, where the roots of the ash trees are particularly large. On one side of the pool is a small waterfall that sends out a soft, soothing, splashing sound. For a moment, the stone in your hand becomes fluid and your fingers move right through it. Its molecules become solid again as you continue to stroke its surface.

Gazing into the stone, you impart the soothing and relaxing feeling of the waterfall into stone. Merging and becoming One with the stone, your fingers reach into its interior, into its very molecules and atoms. Using expectation, desire, and merging, you move the awareness of the waterfall into the stone. You merge with Oneness and feel yourself diffusing into a cloud of boundless energy and light. At this point, the stone becomes a talisman, permanently imprinted with the energy of the waterfall.

Forever-beginning, forever-ending, ever-growing, and ever-flowing are the energetic qualities of Oneness. As you merge, experience this divine connection and tap into this sea of potential energy. Enter into a relationship of energies, where you are simultaneously yourself and more than yourself. Allow yourself to bathe in this energy for a few minutes.

Slowly moving your hands, toes, and feet, you come back to the present moment. You feel the stone, which is now a talisman, still in your hand. At any time, you can take out your talisman, and no matter where you are, through the talisman you can feel the soothing waterfall in the garden. Carry the stone with you and whenever you feel stressed, take out your talisman and use it to feel more relaxed and refreshed.

The Second Magickal Work— The Pentacle

Today the pentacle or five-pointed star is as popular a symbol as the peace sign was in the 1960s! In the Celtic Druid tradition, the upright pentacle designates first degree. A double pentacle, one upright and one reversed, designates second degree. Two interwoven pentacles, one upright and one reversed, surrounded by one to three circles, designate third degree and craft mastery. (See examples on pages 82 and 83.)

Used to invoke divine energies, to seal, and for magickal protection, pentacles come in all shapes and sizes. Traditionally handmade, painted, carved flat disks of wood, metal, or glass, they are frequently worn as jewelry, placed on altars, and hung over doorways and windows. Pentacles occur in nature such as the sand dollar or starfish.

In Celtic Druidism, the pentacle is used to attain your goals and to obtain things, not to manipulate people and not as a form of adornment. Before doing the pentacle, be certain you know what it is that you want, and that you really want it! Remember that an error in calculation will result in an error in situation. For this reason, imagine what it will feel like to attain your goal, and how it will influence your life and those around you.

Your goal needs to be SMART:

+ **S**pecific: Identify your target.
+ **M**easurable: To let you know how close you are to attaining your goal.
+ **A**ttainable: Out of reach, but not out of sight.
+ **R**ealistic: A real chance of reaching your goal.
+ **T**imely: An accomplishment point or timeline for achievement.

Your first pentacle needs to be a goal you know you can attain. This helps you understand the pentacle process and gives you the payoff of success, which provides incentive for you to try again. Set your expectation in place, fixing a clear image of your goal in your mind. Give this image rich detail and color. Remember the clearer your expectation and the stronger your desire, the more energy you will be able to direct toward your goal.

Instructions for Doing the Pentacle

Use the following steps to make your own pentacle. Read the instructions a couple of times, and then gather together the items you need before doing the magickal work.

1. Write your specific goal on a sheet of paper. Make sure it is clear and concise. Work with one goal at a time.

2. State your goal aloud three times.

3. Write down the steps for attaining your goal. Keep these steps simple and to the point. Delete all unnecessary words.

4. On another sheet of paper, make up original symbols for the concepts in your goal and list of steps. For example: I want a house.

I want

A house

Money

Get loan

Continue through the list. If a concept is repeated, use the same symbol for it each time.

5. It is very important that you memorize the symbols so that when you look at a symbol, the associated concept will instantly come to mind.

6. Do steps 1 to 6 of the Nine Steps of the Ritual of a Magickal Work.

7. Ask deity to help you with your pentacle. Do this by calling a specific Celtic Goddess or God into your circle, and requesting their blessing, guidance, and protection. For example, say, "Ayea, Ayea, Anu. Ayea, Ayea Dagda. Ayea, Ayea, Ayea! Please guide, bless, and protect me and this work. Blessed be!"

8. On a large sheet of paper or poster board (at least 2' x 2'), draw a large five-pointed star. I recommend using a felt pen with a thick tip so your image stands out.

9. Into point #1 (head), draw the symbol that you have chosen to represent you.

10. Into point #2 (arm), draw the symbol(s) that represent your goal.

11. Into points #3 and #4 (legs), draw the symbols that represent the steps you will take to attain your goal.

12. Into point #5 (arm), draw the symbols of attaining your goal. This represents the successful outcome. The outcome needs to satisfy you and those affected by it.

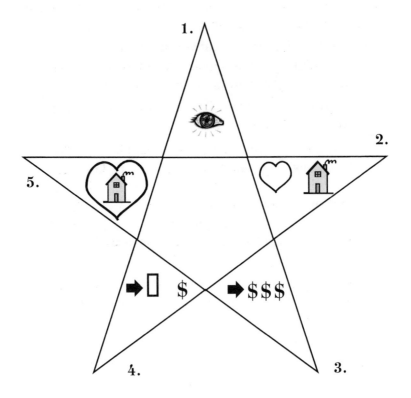

13. Hang the chart at eye level where you can easily see it.

14. Hold your wand in front of you, and breathe deeply for a minute, breathing in to the count of three, holding your breath for three counts, and then breathing out to the count of three.

15. Merge via emotion, music, dancing, or whatever method you prefer.

16. Beginning at the head of the pentacle, hold your wand in your power hand (for example, right if you are right-handed), and point it at the symbol in the topmost point #1, or "head" of the pentacle. Your wand tip should be about six inches from the chart's surface. Move your wand clockwise in a circular pattern around the chart, and imagine the symbols flashing through your mind, one at a time. energetically connecting points 1 to 2 to 3 to 4, and finishing at point 5. Next, imagine a bright green thread coming out of the tip of your wand, and weaving the head, arms, and legs of the pentacle into one. Repeat this three times.

17. Breathe deeply and then imagine releasing thought energy so powerful and complete that this energy shapes reality and your goal is actualized. Know this to be true.

18. Put your wand down, and clap your hands loudly.

19. Turn around and leave the area for a few minutes. Your pentacle is done.

20. Thank the Goddess and God who helped you with your work.

21. Pull up your circle, and put everything away. To help focus your energy on attaining your goal, I recommend leaving your pentacle chart on the wall.

22. Immediately begin to take the steps represented by the symbols in the legs of your pentacle. You must take these steps to complete the work and attain your goal.

When I did my first pentacle work, I remember feeling lightheaded, as if I were floating. When I was moving my wand around the pentacle for the third time, it felt as if I had entered a gap in time where everything came to a stop and then started up again. I left my pentacle chart on the living room wall for about four weeks until I attained my goal.

Pentacle Visualization

A pentacle visualization I learned while in rapport with deity is to imagine yourself merging into and becoming the head and limbs of your pentacle, and then transforming into a star of light. Do this visualization technique just as you drift to sleep or just after waking up. These are the two times of the day when you are most suggestible.

Begin by imagining yourself standing next to a small mountain creek on a warm Summer afternoon. Your attention flows down towards a bright star reflecting in the water of the creek. At almost the same instant, you glance upward as four mountain jays fly above you and finally perch on the tall rowan trees. The birds look like glistening blue jewels of the forest in the growing morning sun. All at once, they begin to caw and whistle, creating a cacophony of noises. You smile and mimic the sounds of the birds back to them. The mountain jays are suddenly quiet, tilting their heads back and forth, watching and waiting.

Returning your attention to the creek, you bend down and put your hand in the water, moving the small stones on the creek bottom ever so slightly. You notice the star-like light emanates from an inch-long clear crystal, and you pick up the stone, pulling it out of the cold water before turning it over in your hand. Sitting down quietly on the warm, grassy creek bank you hold the stone in your hand, turning it over in the sunlight, and watching as rainbows of color wash through it. You take the pointed crystal and begin to draw a five-pointed pentacle star in the sandy bank of the creek.

Into the head, arms, and legs of the pentacle, see and sense yourself drawing the symbols of your deepest desires in the soft soil. Setting the crystal point next to your pentacle of Earth, trace your fingers along the carved pattern and symbols in the soft sandy soil, merging with the symbols and Elements: the Earth, the water of the creek, the trees, bluejays, sunlight, and the cooling breeze. You notice the afternoon has turned into evening and the stars are just beginning to come out.

As you sit next to the soft running creek, allow your emotions to permeate your pentacle, moving the energy outward toward the attainment of your innermost desires. Move ahead in time and space, and see and feel yourself as already having achieved the successful attainment of your desires. Merge as deeply as you possibly can, and then make an effort to merge even deeper. Breathe in to the count of three, hold your breath for three counts, and then exhale completely. Do this three times, and then merge even more deeply.

See your pentacle as a complete success. Create a compelling future—something that draws you toward it, and in your mind picture or sense an inner theater. Picture where you will be and where the action is, feeling the feelings and doing the doings. See or sense the images unfolding in a positive way. Choose a bright, colorful, and exciting outcome to your magickal work.

Allow yourself to cast your deepest desires into the symbols and pentacle of Earth. In your mind's eye, see or sense yourself energetically pulling up the pentacle from the creek bank as if it were a star of white light, edged in cobalt blue. Clothe yourself in this star of white light, covering your head, arms and legs with the luminous pentacle, until you become a brilliant disk of light.

Send your awareness and star body out over the creek, over the tops of the trees, and into the evening sky. Fully transform yourself into a luminous star pentacle. Move as a star on the surface of the night sky, spinning softly as you fly out across the expanse. See and sense yourself being filled completely with white starlight. Breathe this light into your being to the count of three, hold your breath for three counts, and exhale slowly. Repeat this three times.

After a few minutes, come back to the present moment by moving your hands and feet and opening your eyes.

The Third Magickal Work— The Binding

When I first presented the binding work, I didn't want to make or use the poppet. I didn't like the idea of tying something to myself or away from myself. After asking about a hundred questions as to the purpose of this work, I finally realized that the binding work was something much different than what I first thought.

Of primary importance, I discovered that you never bind yourself to another person or bind anyone to you. Traditionally, that is strictly forbidden and extremely unwise. You are manipulating another individual when you do that, again something that is strongly frowned upon by the Druid tradition, as well as by most other mystery traditions. It is essential to influence events with your magickal field of intention rather than manipulate other people. The only time you bind someone away from you is if that person is doing you or your family physical, mental, or spiritual harm.

Through experience, I have found that the best thing to bind yourself to is your higher self and harmonics of light, especially the green harmonic of growth, healing, and abundance. Before binding yourself to the green harmonic, I suggest reading the instructions over a couple of times. Then gather together the following items:

✦ **A yard of green ribbon, twine, yarn, embroidery thread, or string**. Yarn or ribbon work best because they are both readily available from most stores. You can buy embroidery thread at fabric stores and green string at most hardware and garden stores.

✦ **A handmade doll (poppet) made from green cloth.** The doll represents your energetic self. This self is beyond the body, boundless and unlimited. Your energetic self exists beyond time and space. The doll is made after you set up your altar and draw your sacred circle.

✦ **A small green stone such as malachite, aventurine, or jade.** Use a small green stone you find in a river bed, at the ocean, next to the lake, or in your backyard; you can also buy a small tumbled stone. New Age stores, educational toy stores, lapidary supply stores, and the Internet all sell tumbled stones.

✦ **A bay leaf.** A fresh bay leaf is best, but a dried leaf will also work.

✦ **Three pinches of dried rosemary herb**. Fresh rosemary, the kind you grow in your own garden, works best. Dried rosemary herb is available at the market.

✦ **Small cut-up pieces of green cloth for stuffing.** Cut the leftover pieces of fabric in small strips for stuffing.

✦ **A chant of binding.** In your chant, mention the name of the person (or thing), why they are being bound, and how long they will be bound.

✦ **A green candle to seal the yarn.** A green taper candle works best for this purpose, but if you prefer, you can use a votive or specially shaped candle.

✦ **An envelope for the doll**. A plain or colored envelope can be used for this purpose.

Instructions for Doing the Binding

The following 13 steps can be used to bind yourself to your higher self and the green harmonic of abundance.

1. Do steps 1 to 6 of the Nine Steps of the Ritual of a Magickal Work.

2. Put the green stone in the bowl of salt water for a few minutes, take it out, and dry it off. This clears the stone of any unwanted energies.

3. Place the stone and the other items listed previously on your altar.

4. Dedicate your binding work to a favorite Celtic Goddess and God of abundance such as Anu and Dagda. Do this by holding the cloth you will be using for the doll and the length of yarn between your hands, and then asking for help with the magickal work. For example, say:

> May Anu and Dagda bless this circle with
>   their presence.
> Great Lady and the Good God, please
>   protect and guide me!
> Blessed be. Blessed be my binding work.
>   So be it!

5. Use consecrated scissors to cut out your doll by doubling the cloth over and cutting out two identical pieces. Sew the two pieces together with green thread with a consecrated needle. In a pinch, you can use a stapler, also preferably consecrated (refer to Chapter 3 for ways to consecrate tools). The doll is about six to nine inches tall. The head, arms, and legs of the doll should be part of your overall design. Hand stitch the doll from the legs up, leaving a opening at the top of the head for the stuffing, stone, and herbs. This is an example of a basic doll design:

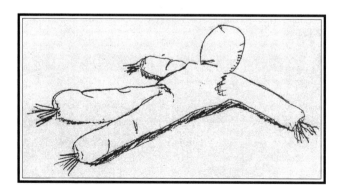

Basic doll design

6. Stuff the body of the doll with the strips of cloth and three pinches of rosemary and bay leaf. Fill it to the neck, and then place the stone in the head and some strips of cloth in the head, and sew up the top. As you are making your poppet, make an effort to focus on binding yourself to the green harmonic of energy and to your higher self. One way to do this is by imagining all the things that are green—the trees, plants, stones, vegetables, and so forth. Imagine all the best times you have experienced, times of plenty, times of enlightenment, joy, and abundance. Use deep breathing and play Celtic or soft instrumental music to help you focus on the work at hand.

7. Slowly wind the yarn around the doll, chanting the words of the binding chant. Say:

> I, [state your given and magickal names],
> Am bound to the green harmonic and my higher self.
> I am bound to the powers of abundance and growth,
> And to my higher abilities and intuitions,
> May it be so until I undo this binding.
> By the powers of the land, sea, sky, and stars,
> I call upon earth, air, fire, water, and deity!
> May you all lend your power to bind this work.
> This is my will. So be it! Blessed be!

As you chant and wind the yarn, imagine the powers of abundance surging through you and into the doll. Use your breath to build the intensity of the energy. Focus on connecting with the green harmonic and your higher self. Keep winding the yarn around the doll and chanting until you have wound the entire length.

8. Carefully drip candle wax, one drop at a time, on the ends of the yarn and the doll to hold the yarn firmly in place. Be careful not to burn your finger, the doll, or the furniture. Use something to protect the surface of your altar such as a piece of cardboard or a plate to catch wax drippings. It may take a few minutes, and several layers, to get a strong seal with the wax.

9. Hold the doll between your hands and say loudly which Goddesses and Gods protect you and your binding work. For example, say:

> My binding work is protected and blessed
> By the Great Mother Goddess Anu and
> the Good God Dagda.
> May the Lady and Lord protect me.
> So be it!

(Note: When binding someone away from you who is doing you harm, state aloud that you are protected against reprisal by the one you have bound, and which Goddess and God protects you and your work.)

10. Hold the doll in your hands, gaze at the images of the Goddess and God on your altar, and imagine binding yourself to abundance and your higher self as you merge as deeply as you can. Use deep breathing to merge even deeper.

11. Imagine yourself being surrounded in a luminous egg of bright green light for several minutes. Breathe in the bright green light, and feel yourself being filled with its positive power. Know that more abundance will flow into your life as your higher self emerges.

12. Put the doll in the envelope. Write your name on it in code, for example in runes, ogham, or Theban, and the date of when you did the work. Also draw or paint a sign of the Goddess such as a star, spiral, or moon on the envelope. You can draw personal symbols or Sigils on it as well. Keep the envelope in a secret and safe place for as long as you want the binding to remain in place.

13. Purify yourself by taking a bath with 1/2 cup sea salt and/or nine drops of lavender oil. Another way to purify yourself is by smudging yourself with sage. After you have purified yourself, put your altar items carefully away.

If you ever need to release the binding, you can do so by disassembling the doll into its component parts. As you do this, chant a simple undoing chant such as "I am no longer bound. So be it!" with the intention of releasing the binding work.

Binding Visualization

Get comfortable by sitting or reclining. Breathe deeply, inhaling and exhaling in slow breaths. With each exhale, you become more relaxed. Feel yourself being cleared and refreshed by a sparkling, pure, stream of white light. The white light spreads out all over your body until your energy feels completely clear.

Now that it's clear and full of white light, feel your spirit begin to soar out of your body. Lighter than air, you float higher, moving out of wherever you are until you are floating high in the sky. Looking down, you see the tops of trees as you float on. In the distance, you see a clearing. As you move closer, you see that it is a green paradise of life.

Beginning to descend into the clearing, you now see it is a beautiful meadow, covered with wild flowers of all colors and shapes. As your feet softly touch the ground, you become aware of the life all around you—the grass, the crickets, and the birds. As you stand in the meadow, you feel connected to the source of all life.

Reaching down, you pick a blade of grass, and stare into its greenness. Putting it up to your nose, you smell its greenness. Now with all of your senses, merge and become all greenness. Green is the color of fertility and abundance.

Now go a step further, and become One with the green harmonic. As you become One, you feel an intimate relationship with the green glowing light. Use your expectation, desire, and merging to make the connection with the light even deeper, becoming one with all that is green. By connecting and binding yourself to the green harmonic, you bring more abundance, fruitfulness, and joy into your life.

You feel yourself returning to your body as you again become aware of your breathing, each breath bringing you back to the present moment. Before getting up, reflect for a moment on your binding to the green harmonic. Assure yourself that you can return to the green meadow at anytime. Know that with a little nurturing, all your goals are well within your grasp.

The Fourth Magickal Work—The Healing Work

Most illnesses and diseases are directly related to unresolved emotional pain and are the result of something you still haven't worked out. Many times illness is connected to negative relationships, either with yourself or others. Suppressed emotional pain often becomes physical pain or sickness, and can even cause premature death.

Each of us is born with natural healing abilities, and we are instruments of the healing light of the Goddess and God. We act as channels for this positive energy. This Druid Ritual of Healing, the fourth magickal work, shows you how to tap into this healing energy and express your natural healing powers.

This magickal work is very effective and uses healing images. You move toward what you picture in your mind, actually imaging yourself into the future. This is important for healing because images influence your emotions (energy in motion). There is a predictable transfer of energy from imagery to reality. Thinking positive images creates a positive self-image, while dwelling on self-destructive images creates a negative self-image.

You will need salt, water, a green candle, incense burner, and athame, as well as two clean sheets of paper, pen, matches, and a small box. Your incense burner needs to be large enough to hold a burning sheet of paper. If your athame is not dulled, make certain the blade will not damage the surface when you excise the disease.

Instructions for Doing the Healing Work

Do this work on a full moon. Follow these directions to do your first healing work on yourself. After you have perfected the work, you can do the work for those you love in need of healing energy.

1. Do steps 1 to 6 of the Nine Steps of the Ritual of a Magickal Work.

2. Dedicate your work to a Celtic Goddess or God of healing such as Bridget or Diancecht.

3. Draw a very basic picture of yourself. Clearly outline the problem area, and write all the particulars of the problem or illness next to the problem area. Highlight the area by circling it. If there is more than one problem or disease, do a separate healing work for each.

4. Take a deep breath, and merge deeply with Oneness for a few minutes.

5. Use your athame to excise the problem or illness, energetically cutting and scraping the problem area, and then carefully using the tip of your athame to cut and scrape the problem area on the paper in front of you.

6. Burn this paper in your incense burner, keeping all of the ashes in the burner.

7. For the Blessing of Health, take a clean sheet of paper and draw another picture of yourself, this time without the problem or illness, making the drawing a little larger. Around and across your image, write down all of the qualities of good health that you desire.

8. Focus on the picture for a few minutes.

9. Chant a blessing of health, over and over. For example,

> May I now be filled with the healing
> power of Oneness.
> By the stars, moon, sun, sky, earth, and
> sea, So be it!

10. Merge with your picture of health in front of you, and become One with it. See and sense the healing being complete as if you were moving into the future for a few minutes and feeling a tremendous sense of well being and splendid health.

12. Return to the present moment, and then say, "So be it! So be it! So be it!"

13. Fold the paper in half, and in half again, and then in half once again, into a small square. Seal it with wax from the candle. Do this over something to catch any drops of wax, being careful to avoid burning yourself, or dripping wax on the furniture and rug.

14. Put the sealed paper into the box, and put the box somewhere safe and secret where it won't be disturbed.

15. Pour the water from your altar chalice into the bowl of salt. Mix it with the index finger of your dominant hand, or with the blade of your athame.

16. Pour the bowl of salt water over the ashes in the censer. The salt purifies, removing all energetic record of the disease from the ashes. Use your athame to stir the ashes counterclockwise three times, being careful not to spill any of the mixture.

17. Take the censor outside, dig a small hole with your athame, and then pour the contents of the censor into the hole. Cover it over. Leave the area looking as undisturbed as possible.

18. Go back inside, face your altar, and loudly clap your hands once.

19. Thank deity, and pull up the circle. Wash all of your tools with salt water, rinse them in cool water, and then dry them and put them away.

Healing Visualization

Lie down or recline comfortably with your arms by your side. Close your eyes and start mentally going down your physical body. Visualize your head, your ears, your eyes, nose, mouth, chin, neck, and so on, down to your toes. As you move through each part of your body, sense how each part feels, and whether there is any discomfort.

As you finally reach your toes, visualize a white thread of light connecting and weaving each part of your body together energetically. Now call in the Goddess or God that you would like to help you in the healing. Personally, I like to use a female and male combination because it adds strength to the healing. Feel the Divine energy of Goddess and God as it enters and becomes part of you.

Now take each part of your body, and go back over it, imparting the divine healing energy of the Goddess and God to each part. After going over each part, then go back and focus on the parts that have discomfort. Use the Divine energy to balance the discomfort, and bring them back into equilibrium. Visualize a healthy body, free of pain and disease. Just be aware of the discomfort until you no longer sense it.

Feel yourself become pure light. Your body, mind, and spirit become One within the spectrum. The blue light spreads out over your body and neutralizes all negativity. Feel all disease within your body being cleared out and neutralized. Again focus on the parts where you have problems, and visualize the blue light pouring over those parts of your body. Use expectation, desire, and merging, to deepen the effect of the healing. Keep bathing your body in blue light until the negativity is washed away.

Next, use green light to impart healthy new patterns into your body. Visualize green light completely covering and filling your body. Feel the healing energy of the Goddess and God flowing through you, building new positive patterns within your body.

Next, feel a brilliant gold light filling your body, empowering you to your fullest. Like the warmth of a sun, it bathes your body in its healing and invigorating warmth. Each part of your body becomes whole again, filled with warm healing light.

For a moment, you move your awareness beyond the confines of your human body into your light body, which knows no pain or suffering. As you become pure light, you leave behind all your physical limitations and move into a boundless Otherworld. In all aspects, you are always light, no matter what your present physical form.

Once more, feel the divine healing light pass over your body imparting each part with its healing energy. Visualize your body as healthy and whole. Keep this image firmly in your mind as you move back to the present moment. See and sense each part of your body as being more alive, feeling more healthy, than it was before.

The Fifth Magickal Work— The Cone of Power

Traditionally, you perform the fifth magickal work, raising the cone of power, for your teacher. Set a special altar for the occasion by adding fresh flowers, plants, music, and other personal sacred objects.

Before you begin the work, you need to be certain as to why you are doing it. Cones are mass amounts of merged energy that are programmed and directed toward a specific goal. For example, you can direct the cone toward practical goals such as getting a better job or buying a house. Or you can direct the cone toward spiritual goals such as healing and global awareness.

Search your heart for your goal and be clear about your reasons for doing the work. Your intention needs to be positive and your desire strong. I suggest you direct the energy of your first cone of power toward healing the wounds of others and the earth. You can do this by sending a bright cone outward in a 10-, 20-, 100-or-more-mile radius, with the intention that divine healing energy fill the people and land.

By raising a cone of power, and then directing it to a chosen destination, you start to realize the immense power of the mind. When you turn your mind, with intention and divine power, toward something long enough, it actually influences the energy and shapes reality. What you turn your mind to is what you bring into your life. This is the basis of the cone of power and all magick. Reality emerges from an ever-changing web of powerful, interwoven thoughts. Everything is structured energy. What structures the energy is your mind.

Instructions for Raising a Cone of Power

To raise your own cone of power, follow these directions:

1. Do steps 1 to 6 of the Nine Steps of the Ritual of a Magickal Work.

2. Dedicate your work to your sponsor Celtic Goddess or God.

3. Use your wand to draw a circle of energy approximately one foot in diameter on the floor in front of you. This circle of energy is not for standing in.

4. Merge with Oneness, and then go deeper into the boundless, letting your body flow away from you naturally as a brilliant violet light floods your mind.

5. Hold your wand in your power hand, high in the air. Face the North point of the circle. Imagine the violet light filling the circle and your being, growing stronger, brighter, and more intense as you slowly spin sunwise (clockwise), from the North to the East, then South, West, and back to the North. Spin three full circles, building the violet light each time you spin around.

6. Stop and face the small circle you previously drew in front of you, and in a commanding voice say, "Ayea, Ayea, Ayea!"

7. Slowly lower your wand, pointing it toward the center of the small circle. Imagine a shaft of white light descending from the tip of your wand and filling the small circle. See it growing more intense, until it is a bright cone of power.

8. Draw up the cone of white light, lifting it in your mind, higher and higher.

9. Finally, when you feel the intensity of the cone is almost bursting, release the cone and direct it where you wish with a great shout, "Go!"

10. Imagine your cone reaching its intended destination for at least a minute or two. Imagine and feel the positive effects of the cone's energy as if you were walking into a tunnel into the future. Be there, and experience the successful outcome of your goal. Bathe in the light and energy for a few minutes.

11. Clap your hands loudly to bring you back to the present moment.

12. Thank your sponsor Goddess or God aloud for their presence, help, and protection. Thank your teacher if she or he is present.

13. Pull up the circle, and put everything away.

Raising a Cone of Power Visualization

Tonight as you lie down to sleep, dream a dream that raises a cone of power that can ignite magickal patterns. The cone of power moves energy from dream reality into physical reality. Visualize what you want, and put all your energy towards that aim. If your aim is true, then nothing will deter you.

You come from light, you are the light, and when you die, you return to light. Light at this point becomes the primary force that moves life. Light and the lack of it is the primary concern of all art and spirituality.

Raising a cone of power visualization is about seeing reality as constructed in patterns or fields of energy, located and connected in time and space. Reality becomes boundless and as such free from the tethers of the time-space continuum, allowing you to fly free through the multidimensional cosmic web.

Imagine the energy flowing, first with a circular motion through your clasped hands, then gradually beginning to move inward and upward to form a cone. Take in energy with one hand while sending it out through the other, creating a balanced and sustainable energy flow. Think of loosing an arrow from a bow; from the moment of release, the arrow moves of its own accord along the course you have set for it, its own power is amplified with the power of the Earth.

Now imagine and feel the energy gathering strength and begin to pick up speed. Imagine directing the cone of energy faster and faster. Feel the cone fill with power and energy from you, your environment, the Earth, the core of the Earth, from the water that flows through the Earth, from the air and sun. Imagine and feel all these elements combine and add power and energy to your cone of power.

Like an ancient God of smithcraft, with the cone of energy you forge a connection with all things, with such intimacy that their breath is your breath, their life is your life. You become the cone and the embodiment of the divine flame, and you build a strong "Cone of Love Power" over the Earth; a magickal cone that connects you with yourself, others, the planet, stars, and the cosmos.

You see the cosmic fabric of light, knowing you are free to follow any thread, which means you are able to merge and create any pattern you truly desire in your life. As your mind explores new dimensions of the cosmos, you see that everything is innately interwoven. Suddenly you understand the power of intent when merging and patterning your world. You realize for your mind to expand, you need to open yourself to your perceptions of realms and Otherworlds beyond ordinary reality.

Raise the cone of power and direct it to a higher purpose of humankind. If we set our sights to the heart of the sun, then maybe we will stay within the light-filled days of the present. Live each day with as much light as you can give. Feel the energy and light flow through your being as you send it out into the universe. Dare to dream a more loving consensus dream for humanity and our Mother Earth.

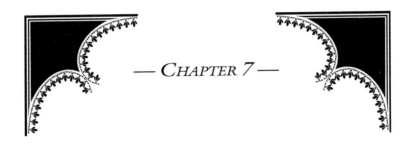

CHAPTER 7

THE FUTURE OF DRUIDISM

At this point in human evolution, a re-emergence of the feminine is taking place. What this means is that people are taking the time to get in touch with their intuitions, and at the same time, developing their spiritual side. This transition also includes everyone getting in touch with their roots, particularly with respects to the Earth and our ancestry as humans moving forever into the future.

Celtic Druidism offers a vehicle for reconnecting with the feminine through the Goddess. It bridges the gap between our past and future. The present represents our progress and, hopefully, forward movement in an evolutionary sense. By bringing the Goddess back into the picture, each of us begins to integrate the male and female energies together into a whole. These energies are an intricate part of life. Integrating these energies into a workable balance is what modern Celtic Druidism is all about.

You wake up every morning, and the world begins to flood in. You are affected and respond to this input in many ways. Sometimes you have to wield your sword and fight, and other times you have to go with your emotions and show compassion. It is the balance of these poles that creates who you are, were, and will be.

Within this context, it is important to focus and direct your energy toward engineering positive patterns of light that are constructive, instead of negative patterns that end in chaos. By beginning to see the whole fabric of light, you understand that you are free to follow any thread, meaning that you are able to merge and create patterns in accordance with your deepest desires.

As your mind begins to explore new dimensions of the cosmos and the human psyche, you perceive the interwovenness of all. You realize that true growth in real magick is having experiences that go beyond your level of imagination. In an instant, you grasp the power that intention brings when you merge and pattern your world. For your mind to expand, you need to open your perception. Perception is the key to unlock the doorways to Otherworlds of experience and knowledge.

As boundaries melt away, your perception evolves. You begin to see the larger picture. Reality moves from two to three to four to multidimensional. The idea in stepping out beyond yourself is to see things as they are, and not in terms of yourself and who you perceive yourself to be. The idea in stepping out beyond yourself is to understand the inner workings of why you do what you do. It's like a mirror. The idea in using the outer and inner polarities is to create a balance or synthesis.

The Re-emergence of the Goddess

Spiritual paths that use the Divine energy of the Goddess in ritual and celebration are growing at a phenomenal rate. Unlike some of the paternal religions, Goddess traditions use both female and male energies when working with the divine. The various Goddesses and Gods represent the many aspects that make up the whole of Oneness.

It is this union that completes the cycle, in people as in all of nature. In the Spring, everything falls in love, mates, and the seeds are planted. The Summer is the time that these seeds grow tall and strong. Autumn is the time of harvest, with Winter as the time of dormancy, building strength, and awaiting the new cycle. Each generation spawns the seeds for next generation. The Druid tradition teaches you to pay close attention and nurture your seeds. You will never be sorry because you will be rewarded with a bountiful harvest.

The Mother Goddess, also called the Earth Mother, is symbolic of the Earth itself. Technology and the Age of Reason has shown many things in a scientific sense, but now it is time to connect back to humanity, including its relationship to the divine. At this point, science and spirituality are becoming integrated into a workable whole.

Our relationship with the Earth is at the core of the newly found integration of science and spirituality. No longer can people and trees be cut down indiscriminately to suit the needs of technology, corporations, and so-called scientific "progress." It is a time of working in cooperation with each other and nature.

The Future of Celtic Druidism

From the mythical bird the phoenix comes the idea that from the ashes of old, spring the seeds of the new. In this case, the seeds of Druidism were originally sown several millenniums ago, but the ideas continue to influence and be relevant within terms of today.

Each era of human development defines the scope of its influence. Sometimes these influences are felt through the centuries, redefined by the generations of the time. Even when seeds are thought to be dead, they arise with renewed vigor, from strength gained by their dormancy.

Celtic Druidism uses ritual, magick, and our connection to Oneness as a means for making our lives more complete. Modern Celtic Druidism and human evolution will continue to follow the path of integration, where eventually everything will be joined in Oneness. God and Goddess are all One. At a certain point in development; we will understand that the male and female polarities are an extension of being divinely human. We must integrate the two in order to become whole.

In closing, I would like ask each one of you to move toward what brings you light and joy, and to move away from people and things that create pain and disappointment. I would like to share my hope with you that we will join together as one people and one world, and create a new, more loving myth of humankind:

> May the Blessing of Light
> Be upon you forever—
> Light within, and Light without
> May all the paths you walk
> Be lighted with peace and hope.

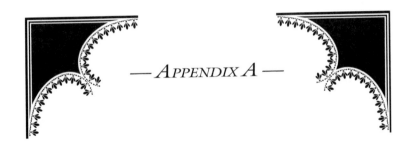

THE OGHAM

Referred to as the Druid Tree Alphabet, the Ogham was devised by the Celtic God Ogma. It was used by the Irish Druids between the first and third centuries C.E. Some scholars think the Ogham is much older, tracing similar inscriptions in Spain and Portugal from 500 B.C.E.

There are 369 Ogham inscriptions that were carved in stone that survive today. They are mostly in Ireland and scattered across Scotland, the Isle of Man, Wales, Corwall, and England, and as far as Silchester (in the Celtic Atrebates). Similar carvings were also found in the state of West Virginia in the United States, which raises the question whether the Celts came to the New World as early as 100 B.C.E.

The Ogham is a system of combining notches (vowels) and lines (consonants) together, which are drawn to, or cross, a baseline or midline called the "whale's back." Each letter consists of one to five slanted or vertical strokes, with vowels designated as notches or dots. The baseline is often the edge of the object on which the Ogham inscription is carved or signed.

You can purchase Oghams or make a set yourself. To make your own set, gather 21 same-sized sticks together. Sand them if you like or leave them natural, and then carve or paint the Oghams on them, one per stick. You can oil them with consecrated oil if you want. This empowers them with the energy of the oil.

Put your Oghams in a fabric bag. Hold the bag between your hands, and then ask for divine guidance. Focus on your question. State your question aloud three times. Draw three, seven, or nine Ogham sticks from the bag without looking at them, or draw three sets of three. Focus on your question once again, and then toss the sticks onto the ground or other flat surface. The sticks landing closest to you represent current influences. Those sticks farthest from you symbolize the future outcome. Any sticks that touch each other are influences that overlap in regards to the question.

Oğham Chart

LETTER	NAME	TREE	THE OGHAM
B	Beith	Birch	
L	Luis	Rowan	
F	Fearn	Alder	
S	Saille	Willow	
N	Nuin	Ash	
H	Huathe	Hawthorn	
D	Duir	Oak	
T	Tinne	Holly	
C	Coll	Hazel	
Q	Quert	Apple	
M	Muin	Vine	
G	Gort	Ivy	
P or Ng	Pethboc/Ngetal	Dwarf Elder/Reed	
Ss	Straif	Blackthorn	
R	Ruis	Elder	
A	Ailim	Silver Fir	
O	Ohn	Furze	
U	Ur	Heather	
E	Eadha	White Poplar	
I	Idho	Yew	
Y	Too sacred to have a name	Mistletoe	

The Ogham Vowels

A - Silver Fir (Ailm)

O - Furze (Onn)

U - Heather (Ur)

E - White Poplar (Eahha)

I - Yew (Idho)

The Ogham Consonants

The consonants are related to the lunar calendar, the festival days, agricultural seasons, and deities.

B -   Birch (Beth)

L -   Rowan (Luis)

N -   Ash (Nuin)

F -   Alder (Fearn)

S -   Willow (Saille)

H -   Hawthorn (Huathe)

D -   Oak (Duir)

T -   Holly (Tinne)

C -   Hazel (Coll)

M -   Vine (Muin)

G -   Ivy (Gort)

P -   Dwarf Elder (Pethboc)

R -   Elder (Ruis)

Q -   Apple (Quert)

Ng - Reed (Ngetal)

Ss - Blackthorn (Straif)

CH - Grove (Koad)

TH - Spindle (Oir)

PE - Honeysuckle (Uilleand)

PH - Beech (Phagos)

XI - The Sea (Mor)

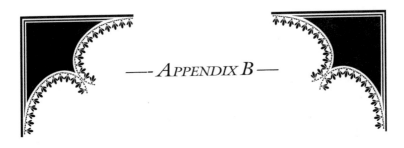

The Elder Futhark Runes

Embodying the secret mysteries of nature, runes are living symbols that offer a profound system of thought and practice that underlies Western culture. Runes act as keys that unlock the mysteries of life. They are tools for communicating with the divine.

Used as alphabets and as tools for divination, the runes originated from the holy signs of the bronze-age magicians, priestesses, and priests. They were threefold symbols (form, idea, and number) that had religious and magickal significance to all who inscribed and used them. The Elder Futhark are the oldest of runes.

The ancients carved runic letters into wood, stone, metal, and bone, and on talismans and grave markers. They used runes for magickal binding, as well as for decorative and symbolic art, house markers, hex signs, and monograms.

Today, runes are useful in magickal works for protection, success, victory, love, and gaining wisdom. You can use runes on your altar cloth, place rune stones on your altar, and inscribe candles with them. It is customary to carve, write, or paint your craft name or the tool's name in runes on your magickal tools. You can do this with consecrated oil if you don't want to physically carve runes on the tool.

The runes that spell out your name can be used as personal power runes. They are your birthright. Check the meanings of the runes in your name to find the runic energies in both your given and craft names. There are no lowercase runes, only uppercase, and no curves, only straight lines, which makes them very easy to learn and write.

The following list of alphabetical correspondences can be used as a general reference when writing runes. Please refer to my book, *The Little Giant Encyclopedia of Runes*, for in-depth information about the runes and their uses.

Alphabetical Correspondences to the Elder Futhark

A–	Ansuz– ᚨ	Ancestral God
B–	Berkana– ᛒ	The Birch Goddess
C–	Kenaz– ᚲ	Torch, Guiding Light
D–	Dagaz– ᛞ	Daylight, Lifting Darkness
E–	Ehwaz– ᛗ	Horse, Twins, Nature
F–	Fehu– ᚠ	Mobile Wealth
G–	Gebo– ᚷ	Gift
H–	Hagalaz– ᚺ	Hail, Cosmic Egg
I–	Isa– | or Eihwaz– ᛇ	Ice or Rebirth
J–	Jera– ᛃ	Good Harvest, Yearly Cycles
K–	Kenaz– ᚲ	Torch, Guiding Light
L–	Laguz– ᛚ	Water, Leek
M–	Mannaz– ᛗ	Humanity
N–	Naudhiz– ᚾ	Need Fire
NG–	Ingwaz– ᛜ	The Earth God Ing, Fertility
O–	Othala– ᛟ	Reward, Ancestral Property, Oneness
P–	Perdhro– ᛈ	Dice Cup, Cauldron, Knowledge
Q–	Kenaz– ᚲ	Torch, Guiding Light
R–	Raidho– ᚱ	Solar Wagon
S–	Sowilo– ᛊ	Sun, Divine Spirit
T–	Tiwaz– ᛏ	Justice

TH– Thurisaz– ᚦ   Thorn

U– Uruz– ᚢ   Auroch/Structure

V– Wunjo– ᚹ
or Uruz– ᚢ   Joy or Structure

W– Wunjo– ᚹ   Joy

X– Kenaz– ᚲ
plus Sowilo– ᚴ   Torch plus the Sun

Y– Jera– ᛃ   Yearly Cycles, Good Harvest

Z– Algiz– ᛦ
or Sowilo– ᚴ   Elk, Protection or the Sun

Final E, Z, or R–
Algiz– ᛦ   Elk, Protection

— APPENDIX C —

THE THEBAN ALPHABET

A	B	C	D	E
F	G	H	I	J
K	L	M	N	O
P	Q	R	S	T
U	V	W	X	Y	Z

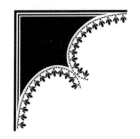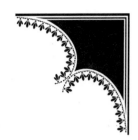

GLOSSARY

All Father: The God.

All Mother: The Goddess.

Art and Craft: The ancient Goddess religion, or Old Religion.

Athame: A two-sided ceremonial knife representing the fire element.

Avalon: Land of the Otherworld, where the Gods live.

Beltane: Great Day at the beginning of May also known as Bel Fire.

Boon Moon: A High Moon, the sixth full moon after Yule.

Boundless: A vast and infinite place of being. See Oneness.

Bridget's Fire: The second Great Day, following Yule.

Bright One: The Bright aspects of the All Mother representing light and life.

Celts: The ancient Gauls and Britons. They were the Welsh, Irish, Highland Scot, Manx, Cornish and Breton peoples of central and western Europe.

Chalice: The ritual tool, or loving cup, associated with the water element and feminine power.

Dark One: The Dark aspect of the All Mother who represents death.

Days of Power: The eight Great Days of ritual celebration.

Elements: Four traditional elements of earth, air, fire, and water, with the fifth element being spirit or the practitioner.

Equinoxes: Solar cycles between the solstices.

Feast: A celebration meal in honor of the Goddess and God.

Four Wards: The four guardians, who stand at the four directional corners (North, East,South, and West) of the sacred circle. Also called the Watchtowers or the Great Wards.

God: An individual being who lives in a merged state.

Goddess: An individual being who lives in a merged state.

Godhood: The attainment of becoming a God. A being who has gone through the three great merges, and moves beyond time and space.

Granting of the Boon: A request of a gift from the Goddess. A boon is a blessing and a gift.

Great Adventure: The continuous cycle of birth, life, death, and rebirth.

Great Book: Also known as the Book of Shadows. A traditional book of teachings and lore said to be over 250 years old, from the Gwyddonic Druid tradition, and copied by hand by initiates.

Great Days: The solstices, equinoxes, and midpoints; Yule, Bridget's Fire, Hertha's Day, Beltane, Letha's Day, Lughnassad, Hellith's Day, and Samhain.

Gwyddonic Druid tradition: A religious and philosophical way to improve your life based on the concept of Oneness.

Hellith's Day: The seventh Great Day celebrating the harvest which takes place on the Autumnal equinox.

Hertha's Day: The third Great Day of the cycle also called Lady's Day, and associated with the beginning of Spring.

High Magick: Magickal works done on the Great Days while in rapport with the Goddess and God.

High Priest: A man representing the God.

High Priestess: A woman representing the Goddess.

Initiation: Being initiated into the art and craft. The birth of one's true self.

Letha's Day: The fifth Great day of the cycle also called Midsummer. A time of complete florescence.

Lughnassad: The sixth Great Day in August that commemorates Lugh's wedding feast.

Mabinogi: A collection of Bardic tales and stories of the lives of the Celtic heroines and heros.

Magickal Tools: Items representing the elements that have been consecrated by a High Priestess and High Priest or by the Goddess and God. They are used to empower ritual and magickal works.

Manifested: Tangible reality.

Merging: The state of becoming One with all things. Diffusing into the boundless.

Negativity: An energetic force which breaks patterns and feeds upon itself. Associated with the Dark One.

Oghams: A form of magickal writing invented by the God Ogma.

Old Religion: The Goddess tradition.

Oneness: The boundless. A state of being where you are connected to all things, nothing, and more, all at the same time.

Patterns: A term for discussing one's expectations and intentions. The foundation from which one merges.

Pentacle: A five-pointed star surrounded by a circle that is used for manifesting and protection.

Positivity: An energetic force which creates patterns. Associated with the Bright One.

Practitioner: A person who practices magick.

Rapport: To be in harmony, friendship, and in close accord with the Goddesses and Gods. The stronger your rapport, the stronger your magick.

Rune: Living symbols with magickal qualities often used in magick.

Salt: It represents the earth element and is used for purifying and clearing energy.

Samhain: All Hollows Eve and the eighth Great Day, associated with ancestry and death. The day when the veil between time and space is the thinnest and you can walk between worlds.

Seeker: A person seeking knowledge about the Art and Craft. The name of an initiate.

Solstice: Time during summer and winter when the sun is at its greatest distance from the celestial equator. Both solstices are Days of Power.

Sunwise: Clockwise turn which is considered the positive direction.

Theban: Ancient form of writing often used in magick.

Three Eyes of Kerridwen: The formula for magick that consists of expectation, desire, and merging.

Threefold One: The Triple Goddess representing birth, life and death.

Tir-nan-Og: Land of Promise, the Celtic paradise.

Tuatha: The family.

Tuatha of Kerridwen: The family of Kerridwen representing the Goddesses and Gods in human incarnate form.

Tuatha De Danann: The family of Danu and title of the Gods.

Unmanifested: Non-tangible reality. That which does not exist as yet.

Wand: The ritual tool representing the air element, traditionally made by the practitioner.

Yule: The first Great Day, celebrated on the Winter solstice.

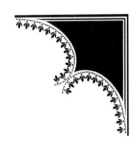

BIBLIOGRAPHY

Bonwick, James. *Irish Druids and Old Irish Religions.* New York: Dorset, 1986.

Bord, Janet and Colin Bord. *Mysterious Britain.* London: Paladin Books, 1974.

Bulfinch, Thomas. *Bulfinch's Mythology.* Garden City, NY: Garden City Publishing Co., Inc., 1938.

Campbell, Joseph. *The Power of Myth.* New York: Doubleday, 1988.

Campbell, Joseph. *The Masks of God, Vols I-IV.* New York: Penguin Books, 1977.

Carr-Gomm, Philip. *The Druid Way.* Rockport, MA: Element Books, Inc., 1993.

Ceram, C. W. *Gods, Graves and Scholars.* New York: Bantam Books, 1972.

Eliade, Mircea. *Shamanism.* Princeton, NJ: Bollingen Series, 1964.

Ellis, Peter Berresford. *The Druids.* Grand Rapids, MI: William B. Eerdmans Publishing Company, 1994.

Ford, Patrick K., Translator. *The Mabinogi and Other Medieval Welsh Tales.* Los Angeles: University of California Press, 1977.

Gaster, Theodor (Editor). *The New Golden Bough.* New York: The New American Library, 1959.

Gimbutas, Marija. *The Goddesses and Gods of Old Eruope.* Berkeley, CA: University of California Press, 1982.

Gimbutas, Marija. *The Language of the Goddess.* San Francisco: Harper & Row, 1989.

Graves, Robert. *The White Goddess.* New York: Faber & Faber, 1966.

Grimal, Pierre (Editor). *Larousse World Mythology.* London: Paul Hamlyn, 1965.

Gruffydd, W. J. *Folklore and Myth in the Mabinogion.* Cardiff: University of Wales Press, 1975.

Jacobs, Joseph (Editor). *Celtic Fairytales.* New York: Dover Publications, Inc., 1968.

King, John. *The Celtic Druids' Year.* London: Blandford, 1994.

Knight, Sirona. *Dream Magic: Night Spells and Rituals For Love, Prosperity, and Personal Power.* San Francisco: Harper San Francisco, 2000.

Knight, Sirona. *Greenfire: Making Love with the Goddess.* St. Paul, MN: Llewellyn Publications, 1995.

Knight, Sirona. *Love, Sex, and Magick.* Secaucas, NJ: Carol Publishing Group, 1999.

Knight, Sirona. *Moonflower: Erotic Dreaming with the Goddess.* St. Paul, MN: Llewellyn Publications, 1996.

Knight, Sirona. *The Pocket Guide to Celtic Spirituality.* Freedom, CA: Crossing Press, 1998.

Knight, Sirona. *The Pocket Guide to Crystals and Gemstones.* Freedom, CA: Crossing Press, 1998.

Knight, Sirona, et al. *The Shapeshifter Tarot.* St. Paul, MN: Llewellyn Publications, 1998.

Leach, Maria (Editor). *Standard Dictionary of Folklore, Mythology, and Legend.* New York: Funk & Wagnalls Co., 1950.

Malory, Sir Thomas. *Le Morte D'Arthur, Vols. I & II.* New York: Mentor Classics, 1962.

Markale, Jean. *The Celts.* Rochester, VT: Inner Traditions International, 1993.

Markale, Jean. *The Druids.* Rochester, VT: Inner Traditions, 1999.

Markale, Jean. *Merlin: Priest of Nature.* Rochester, VT: Inner Traditions, 1995.

Markale, Jean. *Women of the Celts.* Rochester, VT: Inner Traditions, 1986.

Matthews, John. *Taliesin: Shamanic and Bardic Mysteries in Britain and Ireland.* London: Aquarian Press, 1988.

Missing Link Newsletter. Chico, CA. Autumn 1991-Winter 1993.

Monaghan, Patricia. *The Book of Goddesses and Heroines.* St Paul, MN: Llewellyn Publications, 1990.

Mormouth, Geoffrey. *History of the Kings of Britain.* New York: E.P. Dutton & Co., 1958.

Newman, Paul. *The Hill of the Dragon.* London: Kingsmead Press, 1976.

Nexxus Newsletter. Whitesburg, KY. Spring 1985-Fall 1988.

O'Donohue, John. *Anam Cara: A Book of Celtic Wisdom.* New York: HarperCollins, 1997.

Paterson, Helena. *Handbook of Celtic Astrology.* St. Paul, MN: Llewellyn Publications, 1995.

Pepper, Elizabeth and John Wilcock. *Magical and Mystical Sites: Europe and the British Isles.* New York: Harper and Row, 1977.

Phillips, Guy Ragland. *Brigantia, A Mysteriography.* London: Routledge and Kegan Paul Ltds., 1976.

Piggott, Stuart. *The Druids.* London: Thames & Hudson, 1976.

Rees, Alwyn and Brinley Rees. *Celtic Heritage, Ancient Tradition inIreland and Wales.* New York: Grove Press, 1978.

Rhys, John, M. A. *Celtic Folklore, Welsh and Manx.* New York: Benjamin Blom, Inc., 1972.

Sitchin, Zecharia. *When Time Began.* Santa Fe, NM: Bear and Company, 1993.

Smith, Sir William. *Smaller Classical Dictionary.* New York: E. P. Dutton, 1958.

Spence, Lewis. *The History and Origins of Druidism.* New York: Samuel Weiser, Inc., 1971.

Squire, Charles. *Celtic Myth and Legend.* Franklin Lakes, NJ: New Page Books, 2001.

Stewart, R. J. *The Power Within the Land.* Rockport, MA: Element Books, 1992.

Stewart, R. J. and Robin Williamson. *Celtic Druids, Celtic Bards.* London: Blandford Press, 1996.

Stewart, R. J. *Celtic Gods, Celtic Goddesses.* New York: Sterling Publishing Co., 1990.

Wilde, Lady. *Ancient Legends, Mystic Charms and Superstitions of Ireland.* New York: Lemma Publishing, 1973.

Yeats, W.B. *The Celtic Twilight.* New York: Signet Books, 1962.

Yeats, W.B. (Editor). *Irish Folk Stories and Fairy Tales.* New York: Grosset and Dunlap, 1974.

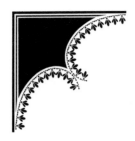
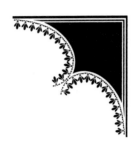

INDEX

— About the Author —

Sirona Knight lives in the Sierra Foothills of Northern California with her family: Michael, her husband of 26 years, and Skylor, their 9-year-old son, four beagles, and a family of cats. Sirona's ancestors include James Smithson, founder of the Smithsonian Institute, and she comes from a long line of the Daughters of the Revolution. She enjoys music, writing poetry, reading, surfing the Internet, as well as homeschooling her son, swimming, watching classic movies, and tending her garden.

Practicing magic for more than 16 years, Sirona is a Third Degree Craft Master of the Celtic Druid Tradition and the High Priestess of the College of the Sun in Northern California. She is the published author of several books on magick, and is the creator and author of the award-winning "Shapeshifter Tarot" deck. In addition, Sirona is a contributing editor for *Magical Blend* magazine. She makes media appearances, both radio and television, and maintains strong Internet visibility through her Web site *(www.sironaknight.com)* by answering e-mail from readers and chatting on Web sites across the United States. Sirona's e-mail address is: bluesky@dcsi.net.

Other Books by Sirona Knight:

Dream Magic

Celtic Traditions

The Little Giant Encyclopedia of Runes

Love, Sex, and Magick

The Shapeshifter Tarot

The Pocket Guide to Celtic Spirituality

The Pocket Guide to Crystals and Gemstones

Moonflower

Greenfire

Forthcoming Books:
A Witch Like Me
The Wiccan Web (with Trish Telesco)
The Cyber Spellbook (with Trish Telesco)
Goddess Bless
Practical Wicca
The Witch and Wizard Training Guide